DATE DUE

NO 16 '87			

PASSAGES IN TEACHING

PASSAGES IN TEACHING

*(Developmental Crises in the Teaching
of Adolescents and Young Adults)*

by

Francis L. Gross, Jr.

Philosophical Library
New York

Library of Congress Cataloging in Publication Data

Gross, Francis L.
  Passages in teaching.

  Includes bibliographical references.
  1. College teaching—Addresses, essays,
lectures. 2. Education—Philosophy—Addresses,
essays, lectures. 3. Adolescence—Addresses,
essays, lectures. I. Title.
LB2331.G77   378'.125   82-3865
ISBN 0-8022-2403-2   AACR2

Copyright © 1982 by Philosophical Library, Inc.
200 West 57th Street, New York, N.Y. 10019

Overseas distributor: George Prior Ltd.
52-54 High Holborn, London WC1V 6RL, England

Manufactured in the United States of America

To the memory of

Rev. William L. Wade, S.J.,
my finest and most contentious teacher,
who never gave me the answers to anything.

CONTENTS

7

PREFACE

Each chapter in this book is a revision of a major essay written in the period of the past ten years. Although each piece has been revised in such a way as to be a part of a single volume, nevertheless I have let the general tone of each one stand. It is to be hoped that such repetition as there is will be an aid rather than a hindrance to the reader.

All of these essays are the fruit of my struggles to find and search the minds of students in a variety of secondary schools and colleges and have stretched geographically from St. John's College in Belize City, Belize to Western Michigan University, where I now find myself. The thoughts in these essays owe a great deal to the men of the Society of Jesus of the Missouri Province, among whom I labored as both student and teacher for more than twenty-five years.

I owe a more recent debt to Dr. Lawrence Israel of the College of General Studies, Western Michigan University. He has been a colleague without whose argumentative companionship most of these pieces would never have been written.

CHAPTER I

THE UNIVERSITY AS ASYLUM

A statement of intent at the beginning of a book seems a modest request, unless of course for artistic reasons one wishes the intent of one's work to appear gradually like a hippo emerging slowly and magnificently from a river. Some intimation of content as well as intent strikes this author as equally reasonable, if one admits that it is hazardous to drastically compress one's expression.

My intent in writing this book is to put developmental psychology to work in the college classroom. I have been intrigued over the years by descriptions of identity crisis, by portrayals of moral development, intellectual development, faith development and other aspects of human development. The question has repeatedly nagged my teacher's curiosity, "How can I use what I know of human development as a teacher?" Sometimes I wonder whether I don't leave my own knowledge of intellectual and ethical development firmly at the door when I walk into my classroom. It is the purpose of this series of essays to bring the insights of several varied developmentalists to bear on the teaching process itself. If I can identify both teacher and student as exemplifying certain stages of development, how does this affect the teaching and learning equation? Can I as a teacher have any effect on the human development of students? Are there ethical implications? Do different developmentalists shed light on one another's theories when viewed from the vantage point of the

COLORADO MOUNTAIN COLLEGE
Alpine Campus - L. R. C.
P.O. Box 775288
Steamboat Springs, CO 80477

teacher? Are there developmental theorists whose very work is so technically written that it needs application and clarification for the teacher?

As a teacher, I have addressed myself to these questions in these ten essays. Since I find it most helpful to write about teaching as a part of my own experience, these essays are often explicitly autobiographical. They are written for other teachers concerned with developmental aspects of teaching. They are meant as well to be straightforward enough to be able to be understood by undergraduate students as well. They are intended, in short, for any adult concerned with the learning process.

We will begin with location, the place where teaching occurs. To attempt a study of process and leave out the environment would be like describing the habits of a tiger while neglecting to mention that the study took place in a zoo.

In this first chapter I refer to large state universities by the word "asylum," a word which admits of a variety of meanings. It is an ambiguous term. It has been used to denote both places of confinement for mentally unbalanced folk as well as a sanctuary affording security and protection for those in need. The purpose of this essay is to see the large state university as a sanctuary for young people. It is primarily concerned with undergraduate students as persons undergoing crises of identity. It seeks to clarify strategies and goals for professors in dealing with these students. The ambiguity of the term "asylum" suggests, however, the possibility that the large state institutions with which we are concerned could indeed become places of confinement, discomfort, and emotional unbalance.

A. The Large State University in 1980

One need not be the sage of the century to note that we live in a time in which natural resources are slim and expensive. The American industrial complex is not a very healthy giant nor a very affluent one. State universities rely for most of their financing on taxes derived by the state from industry. Our tower of learning is threatened by lack of funds as well as a slowly diminishing number of young people emerging from secondary schools, due to declining birth rates.

The tower, however, is built and staffed. Moreover, it is a part of the American dream that higher education be there for all those who want it. Because our tower is a sacred tower, a holy place, we seek to keep it in business. In doing so we run the risk of making it as puzzling a structure as the tower of Babel was some years back in our heritage.[1] There is the risk of a confusion of tongues as well as purpose. The students occupying our sacred tower are changing.

B. The Students: Greater Diversity and Identity Crisis

State university undergraduates have traditionally been a group of people almost as varied as the population of the state.[2] They are becoming more varied still, for we are becoming less restrictive in our enrollment of undergraduates. There are fewer students to choose from. Keeping up enrollment helps keep funds coming from state legislatures now short of funds for reasons indicated earlier. Are our new students dumber than their predecessors? Or are they just different? There is pressure, of course, not only to enroll students but to keep them enrolled. To keep them enrolled they must be given passing grades. Grades, across the country as a matter of fact, are spiralling upward.[3]

I should like to make a case for utilizing the ever more varied richness of our student population rather than regarding that population as folk speaking the babble of the famous tower, incomprehensible to their professors and a millstone around the neck of the institution.

I should like further to note that, in addition to the variety with which we are confronted, there is a certain sameness. Most of our students are still adolescents or young adults. Most of them are well into what Erik Erikson has called a crisis of identity.

Dr. Erikson observes that this crisis

> ...occurs in that period of the life cycle when each youth must forge for himself some central perspective and direction, some working unity, out of the ef-

15

fective remnants of his childhood and the hopes of anticipated adulthood; he must detect some meaningful resemblance between what he has come to see in himself and what his sharpened awareness tells him others judge and expect him to be.[4]

Speaking of this central crisis of integration, Erikson has noted a need for a period of moratorium, a time of relative freedom in which to integrate the identity elements ascribed to the earlier stages of human development in his classic eight stages of the life cycle.[5] Given the Eriksonian stance that such a central period of crisis often occurs or is in the process of occurring during the undergraduate years at a university, I shall complete my characterization of the undergraduate student of today. Four famous young students from the past will hopefully shed light on my description of today's undergraduate. All four have been selected because they lived their student years in times of change and uncertainty, not entirely different from our own time.

C. Four Students in Crisis

The era of the Reformation of Europe provides us with two of these students, both of whom became central in the religious and social changes of their times, both of whom owed in large part their own personal period of integration to the institutional protection of the university framework.

The story of the Basque mystic, evangelist, and Catholic reformer Ignatius of Loyola provides a fascinating study in the role of the university during his own period of integration and identity formation, called by James Brodrick, "the pilgrim years."[6] A gentlemen-soldier, struck in the leg by a cannonball in a battle in the year 1517, he embarked on an inward journey which carried him by stages from the Spanish monastery of Montserrat,[7] to Palestine,[8] to the University of Barcelona, Alcala, Salamanca, and finally the celebrated University of Paris. That his university education began at the age of thirty-three,[9] and ended a full ten years later[10] with the conferral of the Master of Arts degree at the University of Paris, is a tribute to what a learned friend of mine once

16

described, with a reference to his education at the Gregorian University in Rome, as "education in reverse." Out of years of study of Latin and nominalistic philosophy strangely tied to the name of Aristotle, emerged a mystic-organizer who led the reform of the Catholic Counter-Reformation and a new spirit of evangelization in Catholic Christiantiy. His celebrated book of "Spiritual Exercises"[11] bears little of the logic of Aristotle, is written in execrable prose, and is the result of Ignatius' own experiential encounters with his God. Ignatius' penchant for organization and leadership, still at least partially visible in the Jesuit Order of today, was not the result of a specialized university course in management. The protection of the university—although, it must be said, he was expelled from all but his ultimate alma mater—provided a covering for a slowly emerging identity formation process that took nearly twenty years from his original abandonment of a career as a very minor soldier-adventurer.

The apprenticeship of a contemporary of Ignatius, Martin Luther, under the aegis of university and monastery, has been well documented by Erik Erikson himself.[12] Son of an ambitious small industrialist,[13] he sought fulfillment of his father's ambition for him as a precocious university student at the University of Erfurt. Graduating as a Master of Arts in his early twenties, he rather abruptly entered a monastery of Augustinian Friars[14] where his period of moratorium began in earnest.[15] It seems strange that a silent son, a somewhat morose and precocious student, a gentlemanly monk, should eventually emerge as one of the most explosive speakers the world has ever known.[16] But the concern here is that two large institutions, the university and monastery, could each in its own way be the birthplace for a young man's discovery of his own true identity.

If Ignatius became a mystic and the father of an immensely powerful religious order under the mantle of a series of institutions of higher learning hardly dedicated to what he did in fact become—if Martin Luther became a theologian of revolution born, in his own words, "by living, nay dying and being damned, not by thinking, reading or speculating"[17]—we may

17

have some inkling as to the uses of our contemporary seats of higher learning in our own equally turbulent world.

Two other figures, whose pursuits of higher learning reach into our own century, may shed further light on the matter: Mohandas Gandhi and Malcolm X.

Gandhi, the originator of militant non-violence, also served a university apprenticeship. It proved instrumental in his fusion of religious belief and political action, and makes him equally as intriguing as his Reformation university colleagues referred to previously. Gandhi is not known to today's world as a famous lawyer. Yet, his pilgrimage from India to London to study civil law and his subsequent practice of law in South Africa are seen by Dr. Erikson[18] as his period of integration. The young Gandhi's experiments with clothing, religion, food and sex, while a law student in London, are a matter of record.[19] What concerns me is that he was able to try on various identities, from which he could construct that which was his own, at precisely the same time that he was engaged in a university framework. I do not wish to make a case that he never used the skills of his profession, for certainly he did.[20] That he could, while learning his trade, forge an identity out of which to use these tools is what intrigues me.

Perhaps an example, however minor, is called for. As a young man in his twenties, recently arrived in London, Gandhi once, rather inappropriately by British standards, was seen standing in the lobby of the Victorian Hotel in London dressed in an immaculate white flannel suit.[21] Erikson remarks of this episode, not without humor:

> ...the white flannel suit represents much more than the wrong choice of clothing by an innocent young traveler; for as we shall see, Gandhi was always highly aware of the significance of clothes as uniforms which might identify at least one's aberrant identity fragments—until he learned to be himself, near-naked.[22]

The later emergence of Gandhi's militant non-violence was indeed emergence of the naked power of the human spirit in contrast to physical force. The world knows the later, powerful, small figure defying the British governance of his people, while wearing nothing but a small white cloth around his loins. To have slowly discovered that powerful symbol of his own identity while a serious student of law speaks to me of the kinds of things students can learn at a university.

But how, indeed, does the searing and violent story of Malcolm X relate to university learning? To some extent his self-told story is not remarkable, considering the sub-culture in which his boyhood years were spent. His father's violent death when Malcolm was a small boy,[23] his years in reform school,[24] his wandering life as a hustler,[25] his eventual imprisonment for armed robbery can be nearly carbon-copied in the case histories of thousands of black convicts in penitentiaries all over the country.[26]

At the age of twenty Malcolm X began a prison term that was seven long years, the years of his moratorium, his reintegration, his awakening to himself as an adult. As his brother Reginald put it at the beginning of Malcolm's term, "You don't even know who you are." The story of Malcolm's awakening and the set of his sense of mission to his people takes place behind prison walls. It was here that he discovered the teachings of Elijah Muhammad,[27] and the world of books.[28] His painstaking and painful reassessment of himself and his people, his own religious convictions, his emergence as an omnivorous reader, took place in a series of large prisons, each of which had a library and afforded a great deal of free time for the inmates. As he himself puts it, "...up to then, I had never been so truly free in my life."[29] His alma mater? In answer to that very question he said, "Books." "You will never catch me with a free fifteen minutes in which I'm not studying something I feel might help the black man."[30] He might have added that a rather unlikely large institution, the prison system for the state of Massachusetts, had provided the institutional mantle in which this great man discovered both himself and his role in life. The essential ingredient was a certain kind of enclosed freedom coming at a time when he deeply needed to unify and create something from the brutal and rich life as a young black con artist he had known before. Indeed, it is the

19

purpose of this essay to probe the strange forms of freedom afforded to young searching people by unlikely but accessible large institutions, with particular attention given to large state universities.

D. Contemporary Undergraduate Moratoria

It is germane to my purpose here to seek to make more precise just what the university as an institution can offer the student who finds him or herself going through the period of moratorium. I hope it will be helpful to the reader to see this period again defined in the words of Dr. Erikson:

> This period can be viewed as a psychosocial moratorium during which the young adult through free role experimentation may find a niche in some section of his society, a niche which is firmly defined and yet seems to be uniquely made for him....
>
> A moratorium is a period of delay granted to somebody who is not ready to meet an obligation or forced on somebody who should give himself time. It is a period that is characterized by a selective permissiveness on the part of society and of provocative playfulness on the part of youth, and yet it also often leads to deep, if often transitory, commitment on the part of the youth, and ends in a more or less ceremonial confirmation on the part of society....
>
> Each society and each culture institutionalizes a certain moratorium for the majority of its young people.[31]

Erikson seeks to pinpoint seven different but related crises likely to occur during this period of moratorium. My purpose is to identify these crises from a positive point of view as occurring within the large university framework with references taken from the four historical figures to clarify the issues. I shall take each of the crises separately, with the understanding that one or another may be more prominent in the life of an individual student and that each student is, taken individually, all of one piece. We may cut them, like a pie, into seven pieces, for purposes of reflection. But the seven slices

20

must always be understood to be a part of one pie. Hence, each is related to each other. Each is connected with each other. Each occurs within a single person. Each division is a brief metaphor, a short parable, which hopes to shed some light on the individual student-person existing for a time in the societal framework of the university. With these admonitions, let me proceed.

1. Temporal Perspective versus Time Confusion

This crucial period Erikson relates to the earliest period of infancy, a time characterized by the development of a certain basic trust or lack of trust.[32] Malcolm X's prison years afforded him a period in which time meant nearly nothing—a seven-year sentence. (Seven is a mystical number for infinity!) Seven years in prison might seem to be just that—an infinite betrayal of trust perhaps, but with many days to assess the matter, as indeed Malcolm did.

The university, like Malcolm's prison period, offers a plethora of days before the conferral of the undergraduate degree. Indeed, the standardization of the futures expected of contemporary adults conspires to make the moratorium period nearly a way of life.[34] A "sentence" of four years or more gives time, at a period when time is often needed—a period of timelessness, a period in which there is sufficient time to try almost anything.

2. Self-Certainty versus Self-Consciousness

Again there is a temporal relation back to the infancy period when a tiny child first begins to awaken to an emerging unique self, with the accompanying pitfalls of shame over this uniqueness or doubt that it exists.[35]

To be able to hide in the omnipresent undergraduate uniform of blue denim can help in the search for self-certainty before one feels it, much as Gandhi attempted to hide as an uncertain immigrant in a white flannel suit, as Luther hid under the cowl of an Augustianian friar, or as Malcolm X was safely protected by the uniform of a prisoner. Uniforms of varying kinds can give one a breathing period, a time of apparent external certainty during which one finds what clothing in a large sense really fits. It covers the shame, doubt, and uncertainty concomitant with the emergence of a unique human being.[36] The contemporary large university scene certainly is, however helplessly, tolerant of student uniforms.

3. Role Experimentation versus Role Fixation

Again, Erikson notes a resurfacing parallel period occurring earlier, at the end of the third year of childhood. The child at this time is characterized by an emerging initiative, concurrent with rapidly increasing motor control, and its accompanying terrible partners of guilt and a stifling conscience.[37] The young adult in this period of delay is often seen as torn between free experimentation in a variety of roles and a neat but death-dealing fix upon a single way of acting.[38] An institution can support or deny such experimentation. I think of Malcolm's vital experiment with Islamic religion while in prison, Luther's terribly intense experiment with religious vows and ordination to the priesthood, Gandhi's initiation to the strange and free-wheeling life of a law student in London. Likewise, the wandering and sundry initiations into university life in Spain and Paris afforded Ignatius of Loyola similar opportunities for experimentation with vital choices in his life.

Here today, I think of fraternities and sororities (both white and black), initiations into the drug and/or beer-drinking culture, the world of the jock and the Jesus Freak, to name but a few groups. A certain submissiveness is demanded on the part of the member, certain rituals, accompanied by a push to action, experimentation in life style. The social unit provides a protective mantle under which to experiment. Even the much despised grade-point average, often so easy to obtain for a sizable number, provides an opportunity for role experimentation if one grants a certain degree of submissiveness to the systematic aspects of the university. In the framework of the larger community it provides respectability; it can be a badge of real academic quality; or indeed, it can be a convenient cover for various experimentations in sundry roles for the student.

4. Apprenticeship versus Work Paralysis

Still another earlier developmental reference is the chronological stage of nursery and early primary school years. This period is seen by Erikson as being characterized by a need to make things, and to make them well.[39] In young adulthood Erikson sees a parallel need for genuine industry, sanctioned by a status of apprenticeship.[40] Such a status could be provided, or at least abetted by a social institution, an institution allowing a certain degree of license to the apprenticeship as well as defining duties and even sanctioning competition.

Both Martin Luther and Ignatius of Loyola enjoyed apprenticeships as offered by the universities of their times, and demanded for the attainment of the degree of Master of Arts. Gandhi's law study in England, as well as his work as a fledgling lawyer with a growing bent for a unique style of circumventing and confronting the law in South Africa, was not a time devoid of intellectual demands of well-defined dimensions. A certain license—first of all that of the privileged status of the student in the university, second of all the nearly legendary British tolerance for social deviance on the part of university students—is an apt measure of institutional apprenticeship. It is true that Malcolm's time in prison can hardly be construed as an apprenticeship in the sense that Erikson has defined it. Interestingly, however, the prison experience did provide him with the leisure for a rigorous apprenticeship in the Islamism of Elijah Muhammad, an institution in itself. Malcolm's neophyte years as a Muslim in prison were years of rigorous examination of his new-found faith as well as active recruitment among his fellow prisoners.

We have already referred to the possible, but by no means demanding, academic apprenticeship afforded by large state universities on the undergraduate level, even including competition for academic grades. Perhaps under the heading of license I should include an overlap of well-defined duties attached to the myriad social, religious, and political para- institutions flourishing on the fringes of official university life. I think of the rigorous apprenticeship of a young Jehovah's Witness attending one of my classes, the seriousness apparent in women determined to attain, whatever the cost, the varieties of skills, knowledge, and moral fiber demanded for certain equality, but not identity, with their male counterparts in the world of work, love and play. The same intense kind of apprenticeship, fathered in a sense by the prison term of Malcolm X, is apparent in black students, both male and female, and spreads far beyond the official and sanctioned guidelines of requirements for the attainment of the academic degree. Further examples, because there are so many, would not serve to clarify the intent of this essay.

I should like to note here that the three crises left for us to examine in the university framework look forward rather than retrospectively. They are portents of crises to come in later stages of individual life as seen in Erikson's developmental scheme.[41]

5. Sexual Polarization versus Bisexual Confusion

The coming crisis of intimacy versus isolation[42] is therefore foreshadowed by a certain confusion as to one's sex, when a young person does not feel him-or-herself to be clearly a member of one sex or the other.[43] It can be characterized behaviorally as an ascetic turning away from sexuality, a concern with what sort of man or woman one might become, and it may include often genital activity without intimacy.

It is of interest to us that all four of our historical examples—Ignatius, Luther, Malcolm, and to some extent Gandhi—chose to concentrate on intellectual, political, and religious preoccupations which precluded genital activity. Sexual abstinence was the pattern of all four. It should be noted, by way of underlining the fact, that we are speaking of a period of delay and integration, that this period of unanimity of practice for these very disparate characters was not permanent. Ignatius remained celibate. Malcolm and Martin both married some years after their period of moratorium. Gandhi, already married during this period, practiced full conjugal intimacy as well as sexual abstinence for ascetical and political reasons in his years of maturity.

The contemporary undergraduate university student I see is

certainly not overburdened on the large university campus with institutionalized sexual taboos. Dorms and student housing leave this area of behavior a matter of personal choice, given certain discretion. Hugh Hefner's ideology of male-oriented ludic sexual activity is tolerated and so is a rising concern with feminism in varying forms, some of which allow women periods of abstinence, periods of homosexuality, or sharply limited genital activity with carefully selected partners. Total abstinence is not prominent and is hard to identify, except among a variety of the Jesus People.

I cannot but think that such a climate is conducive to the development of an emerging consciousness of intimacy and sexual activity which will go beyond, or at least take into account, the technology that has so changed and controlled the effects of sexual intimacy. The anonymity of large universities is playing a part, however unwittingly, in this potential emergence.

6. Leader- and Followership versus Authority Confusion

Again we look forward to a stage in life identified by Erikson as generativity versus stagnation,[44] primarily concerned with establishing and guiding the next generation. In youth we can see a prescience or anticipation of this stage, a step towards generativity, a learning to assume leadership as well as learning intelligent followership. Such learning portends later values and attitudes.[45]

Leadership and followership demand a cause. Malcolm's cause was his own black people's loss of corporate identity. Gandhi sought freedom and dignity for his own people. Both Luther and Ignatius were concerned with establishing a rock-bottom authenticity to prayer and spirituality as institutionalized by the Christianity of Western Europe in the sixteenth century. All four of these men were groping for ways to establish and nurture their own particular people and the generations that were to follow them.

Each had to learn to lead as well as to follow. Malcolm's struggle to be at once a follower of his own emerging self as a black American as well as a follower of Elijah Muhammad was a struggle indeed. Luther attempted to follow his father, his academic discipline, his religious superiors, and his church, in conjunction with the often opposing rock-bottom convictions he arrived at in his study, and above all, in his prayer. His moratorium provided a period in which he changed from a man who was silent and blindly obedient to an explosively verbose man,[46] a leader of religious revolt, obedient only to his own rock-bottom experiences in prayer. Ignatius turned from being an obedient soldier to being a spiritual leader who taught his men to trust their own experience in prayer as the guiding force of their destinies, just as he had trusted his. Gandhi fused non-violent religion and politics within himself, trusted both his religious upbringing and his expertise in law, and became both an intelligent follower and a unique leader.

How does the university structure provide aid in leadership and followership for students? The university community is fraught with causes—social, religious, academic, and political. It is again the variety that strikes me: a chance for the student to match his-or-her own emerging self with serious, if often temporary, commitment to attempt intelligent followership and/or leadership in anticipation of their future generative stance toward the young people to come in their wake.

7. Ideological Commitment versus Confusion of Values

The role of ideology in the life of the university student undergoing a period of moratorium, related as it is to Erikson's final period of integrity versus despair,[47] encapsulates nevertheless all that we have observed under various headings earlier in this study. It is important, then, in an Eriksonian framework of thought to understand what we mean by the term "ideology."

> We now come to that system of ideals which societies present to the young in the explicit or implicit form of an ideology. From what has been said so far we can ascribe to ideology the function of offering youth (1) a simplified perspective of the future which encompasses all foreseeable time and thus

counteracts individual "time confusion;" (2) some strongly felt correspondence between the inner world of ideals and evils and the social world with its goals and dangers; (3) an opportunity for exhibiting some uniformity of appearance and behavior counteracting individual identity-consciousness; (4) inducement to a collective experimentation with roles and techniques which help overcome sense of inhibition and personal guilt; (5) introduction into the methods of the prevailing technology and thus into sanctioned and regulated competition; (6) a geographic-historical world image as a framework for the young individual's budding identity; (7) a rationale for a sexual way of life compatible with a convincing system of principles; and submission to leaders who as super-human figures or "big brothers" are above the ambivalence of the parent-child relation. Without some such IDEOLOGICAL COMMITMENT, however implicit in a "way of life," youth suffers a CONFUSION OF VALUES...which can be specifically dangerous to the fabric of society.[48]

Our four figures from history can illustrate the role of ideology. Malcolm X needed the simplified perspective which the ideology of Elijah Muhammad offered him during his period in prison. It gave him a base, a source of trust, a springboard for investigation and synthesis for his own emerging identity. His mature years show a slowly growing realization that the vision of his leader had been naive, although Malcolm never lost the rock-bottom faith of his belief in Islam. Perhaps his visit to Mecca, shortly before his death, in which he discovered that people with white skins were not all devils,[49] as well as his discovery of Elijah Muhammad's duplicity concerning his own sexual life and the strictness he preached to his followers are the most poignant evidence of this growth in Malcolm.[50]

Gandhi's slow transformation from religious belief to social action of a political nature never lost the base of that religious belief.[51] Slowly he fused political action with religious practice into militant non-violence. If one may somewhat treacherously call Gandhi's religion the ideology which sustained him as he grew, it would not be far from the mark to say so. One must understand his religion not as a crutch solely. Rather it was a tool which in itself was transformed into a new sphere—that of political action.

Ignatius of Loyola's religious beliefs, ideological as they were,[52] were the bedrock of his experimentation with mysticism[53] and his emergence as a religious leader. His church was a "big sister" whom he followed loyally, fought with and for with great intensity.

Martin Luther's early struggle for commitment was, like that of Ignatius, anchored in Catholic ideology.[54] That he once said in his mature years, "A fart in Wittenburg could be heard in Rome,"[55] is only evidence that he had an institutional set of values out of which to work, experiment, and develop a world image. If his final submission was only to God, the submission to his former religious rule, his father's memory, and his former church, provided the base for his emergence as a leader not notable for his submission to man.

In returning to the contemporary university campus in search of ideology of an institutional nature, I for one find little homogeneity. The simplified world view of which Erikson speaks reduces to, "You Can Get Anything You Want at Alice's Restaurant," to quote Arlo Guthrie. One does find pockets of academe in which professors or departments pursue truth for its own sake. One finds vital concern for social issues from black pride to feminism, among students, faculty and administration. To say that the university offers a simple world view to the student, unless it be something like, "Everything will be somehow better when you graduate," would be a vast over-simplification.

It is the very diversity of dogma and ideology that concerns and fascinates me. The drug culture, the neo-mystics, the feminists, the jocks, the technocrats, environmentalists, the Jesus Freaks, the ethnic Catholics provide only a sampling of

28

ideologies. They provide not so much an overarching world view as a smorgasbord.

It is at this varied table that the student may pick, test, and temporarily make his or her own frame of reference for a moratorium period. Whether students in large part will pick none, and thus provide a good basis for being permanent drifters or automatons in later life, is by no means clear. From an Eriksonian stance it is clear that to a student, engaged in the laborious process of "getting my shit together," some ideology is needed for that operation to be a success.

The initiative, in meaningful and extensive form, has not been taken by the universities. They are too big and too diverse for that. It is our hope that this very bigness will provide a protective if unknowing mantle for some young men and women to choose an ideology out of which they may assess the challenge offered them during the moratorium period— "What have I got and what am I going to do with it?"

E. The Professor: Strategies for Teaching

The reader will note at this juncture that we have talked of university structure with reference to the student during his or her moratorium period. We have illustrated by way of clarification four young men who found integration and education in large structures at varying times and circumstances. Precious little has been said about the professor. In point of fact, the structure as presented seems to leave the professor in limbo, a sort of appendix, contributing little to the integrative process of the student. Such is not my intent, although as a professor I do think that those who really want to learn something will indeed do it with or without us. Are we to be unnoticed voices shouting wisdom amid the varying tongues of the Tower of Babel? It is indeed possible. It is also possible that today's Babel-like structure lends itself to a teaching style that may be effective. I offer some reflections with reference to the Eriksonian seven-fold division of the period of life characterized by identity crisis and moratorium in the structural framework previously described. I think most

29

of these reflections will center around two key concepts, that of the development of a community within the individual classroom, and that of a style of course which may be called problem centered.

When one considers temporal perspective in the classroom, the student can well interpret delays in feedback from the teacher as betrayal. For this reason I advocate frequent testing on a regular basis. Very short individual quizzes or longer group efforts can build trust between teacher and class. Among the students themselves the opportunity of a community of trust within a classroom can be offered by having the class work in small groups of four to six persons during the classroom periods. The attempt, in terms of trust, is to establish a climate of cooperation rather than an unduly competitive situation. Allied to this, by the nature of the small group itself, is an opportunity to express one's self without the undue time delay so often seen in Eriksonian theory as equivalent to betrayal. For an introduction to the small group as an effective learning device, I refer the reader to Chapter Two of this book.

I would add that working in small groups speaks also to the crisis of self-certainty versus self-consciousness. The small group can provide a certain kind of cover, reminiscent of student uniforms. Such cover can provide the uncertain student with a certain security, a certain willingness to take risks and to experiment in his or her work, a well-known phenomenon in the psychology of small groups, known in the trade as the "risky shift" phenomenon. A certain freedom to experiment with different roles within a small group, especially if it is encouraged by the professor, seems obvious. One can attempt leadership or followership in a variety of ways depending on the various environments that make up the group, the task assigned, one's individual expertise and experience in various matters, and one's ability to analyze. Briefly put, a group of forty students divided into eight groups offers a greater variety of active roles as well as actual chances for engaging in the leadership and followership seen by Erikson as so crucial during the moratorium period.

A certain apprenticeship, a spirit of industry, characterizes a cohesive group. Too often as a teacher, I am confronted with students who simply become paralyzed with regard to work. I grant that there are many factors involved, but I submit that given a potentially interesting subject matter, a small group may be a powerful lever for overcoming this paralysis. Sometimes students need a push, literally, to get into the subject, to groove on it, to overcome the space between themselves and what they may well immerse themselves in, given the push. A small group may provide that push. It may provide them with a chance to avoid bad followership (the blind conformity to the all-powerful, all-knowing teacher), or a chance to throw their own weight around, a certain license, if you will.

It is of interest to me that groups of mixed sexes often discover new ways of relating to their own sexuality. Male students working with female students often find themselves for the first time in their lives relating to females as co-workers instead of playmates. If there is a male or female bias it surfaces in work-interaction differently than it does in play-interaction. A young woman, confronted with a difficult task in a group, may discover that she can be, at one and the same time, a leader and a woman. The difficult task with which the group is confronted can cut through a lot of both male and female stereotypes. The task demands solution. A female accustomed to being ogled by her male confreres just might find that she is the only one in the group that can pull them together in a difficult task demanding powers of analysis that she alone in the group possesses. A male, confronted with a fractious group, may discover that he alone can act as the gentle peacemaker. In short, a working group of mixed sexes can often discover in a demanding team situation new aspects of their sexuality. Last, but not least, this new aspect might well be appreciated by the group, for it helps get the job done. As teacher, I am going to grade that job. Most students appreciate good grades, regardless of how they got them.

After discussing sexual roles, so often involving ideological stereotypes, another point of crisis seems appropriate to men-

31

tion, that of ideological commitment. We have discussed, earlier in this paper, a need for ideological commitment as being especially acute and all encompassing during the years of identity crisis. From the point of view of the teacher, such a need cannot be overlooked. To try to teach a value-free discipline makes about as much sense to students as describing God as a triangle. They are searching for commitment. They are testing values worth living for. I feel that an undergraduate course must begin with a problem that confronts them as persons. I don't care whether the subject matter is hard physical science, the social sciences, or that vast array of subject matter that has traditionally come under the heading of humanities. It does not matter whether one is struggling to teach basic English, writing skills or advanced mathematics. What they are searching for is an ideology to test, refine, and live by. If there is no real connection between my biology class and this search, there will be only scattered genuine enthusiasm. At this period of life an approach to teaching which espouses knowledge for its own sake just won't wash.

It is not my purpose here to show just how any given body of knowledge relates to ideological commitment, but a single example of my own field might help. If I am to teach the demanding socio-psychoanalytical theory of Erik Erikson, I could take the stance that any educated person in today's world should know something about psychoanalytical theory as part of the mind furniture of an educated person, a college graduate. Then I just do my level best to cram it into my students and hope that some of them will find it interesting.

On the other hand, I could take a book by Erikson concerned with identity and youth and bluntly say, "This man is talking about you." Then with this as my central drive, I would hope to teach the language and method of this psychologist. Students will not understand what he is saying about them, unless they become acquainted with how he works, how he thinks. Such an approach is value-laden and can lead toward a synthesis of values by which a student may live. Without this pointer to where the student is now, I do not think I could effectively teach the theory, nor would I find it very interesting to do so.

If my one example seems to be a bit too apt a subject to teach in a value-laden and problem-centered approach, let me at least indicate some others. A study of ancient Middle-Eastern literature and history involving, say, the Biblical character of Abraham may remain sterile unless approached from the vantage point of Abraham as a man struggling with the problems of religious belief. In such a course it might be well to say, "That man is you!" A study of biology might well be framed in the ambience of contemplative wonder for the intricacies of the world of living things. A sense of contemplation and marvelling has to do with a personal value. The implication for the destruction of life, the precarious balance of natural organisms so easily thrown off by the tinkering of humans, is another value-laden and problematical issue that can touch the individual student.

Lest such an approach be seen as a selling out of solid technique, a cheap moralizing under the name of psychology, history, biology, or whatever discipline, I ask only why should this be so? I see it as an honest motivational factor, truly educational in itself, which could well drive a student into the hard work of mastering, or delving deeper into, the field in question and indeed out of that field into others.

And so, I say in conclusion, here in our Tower of Babel, amid a richness of different student languages, in a truly gigantic if respectable structure, the teacher might well confront and use those differing student voices, that very impersonality, that permissiveness. I suggest courses that are problem-centered, value-laden and built around small group learning technique. The use of small groups in undergraduate teaching, then, is the subject of the next chapter.

CHAPTER II

USING SMALL GROUPS IN UNDERGRADUATE TEACHING

A. Teachers and Students

An old man once told me when I was a student of philosophy at St. Louis University, "Francis, never trust a successful teacher." A very successful college professor of mathematics once told me later, "Most teachers talk too goddamned much." I have puzzled over these seemingly strange comments on teaching for the past twenty years. They are the genesis of this paper.

With regard to the "successful" teacher, Herbert Kelman sheds some light on why it is possibly a very bad idea to be successful.[1] He identifies three models of social influence on opinion change—compliance, identification, and internalization. Within the classroom perspective I interpret his study as saying that the teacher who demands total compliance must be present to enforce it upon the students. The teacher who is charismatic is also heavily dependent on physical presence; students tend to identify with this teacher primarily and run the risk of parroting whatever he or she says as long as they are close to this person; personal attractiveness is the key. An agent (teacher) who relies neither on the rod nor personal attractiveness is a more likely agent of truly internalized and lasting change. I do not mean to erect a universal model of good teaching by quoting Dr. Kelman. I do hope to shed some light on the remark about successful teachers quoted at the beginning of this essay.

35

As regards most teachers talking too much, I have learned by bitter experience that a clear exposition of my subject matter can often be counterproductive. A great deal of activity on my part, however clear, may be merely soporific from the point of view of the students. Thomas Aquinas long ago pointed out that learning takes place only if the learner does something. One cannot pour knowledge into the head or heart of a student as one pours wine into a glass.[2]

It is not my purpose here to investigate how a lecture can be presented in such a way as to make it more likely that students will become actively involved in it. Work introducing show business techniques into serious teaching is being done, however, by John Ware and his associates.[3] I am not directly concerned with Personalized Systems of Instruction. I am concerned here with a possible answer to the charismatic teacher dilemma as well as the teacher who talks too much. My area of solution is the use of small groups within the larger classroom group.

Let me define more closely the student population I must deal with. As a professor in the College of General Studies in my university, I deal with groups of thirty or more students. There is no General Studies major at the university. All students wishing to obtain a Bachelor's degree must take a certain number of courses in general studies, regardless of the degree program in which they are involved.

This means I am confronted by a wide variety of students—engineering students, aspiring poets and dancers, behavioral psychology majors. There is a wide range in intelligence and cultural background as well. They vary in age, nationality, race and interest. One could say that the only common bond held by all is that they are pursuing undergraduate degrees at Western Michigan University. I grant, as I have noted in the previous chapter, that most of them are living the years between childhood and adulthood, termed by Erikson the time of the crisis of identity.

Financial pressure on the university has caused university administrators to warn us that the ratio of students to teacher will become larger than smaller. The likelihood of teaching a small group of students who already know each other and who share common cultural and intellectual backgrounds is nil. My concern is to admit realistically that I must perforce work with large groups. It is also incumbent upon me to use positively the population that confronts me. There is a richness, if it can be tapped, for purposes of learning.

B. Using Small Groups in Teaching

There is solid empirical evidence that small groups of people can learn better than they could working as individuals, working alone.[4]

It is obvious that the application of such evidence depends on the physical surroundings of the group, the population involved in the group, and the nature of the matter to be learned.

From the outset we must understand that the literature on which we are basing these musings defines a small group as "two or more persons who are interacting with one another in such a manner that each person influences and is influenced by each other."[5]

1. Physical Surroundings

When I consider the physical surroundings of the group as part of the environment of the group, I find the following elements to be of some importance. These elements are mentioned in the literature of the psychology of small groups, but we must remember that we are limiting ourselves to undergraduate general studies courses in a large university.

Territoriality. Any seasoned teacher knows students tend to settle in a particular spot in a classroom, given the chance. Small groups tend to do the same thing. They develop a "turf," much as do teen-age gangs, and will resist being moved from it.[6] For a teacher working with groups to attempt to move the groups, for example, to provide a neater arrangement of space will likely be a needless expense of energy both for him or her as well as the group. They will resist it. Not only that, but the teacher will be likely missing out on a valuable means for identifying the group and its corporate personality;

generally, groups form in places that fit them. A group I recently worked with chose a small alcove in the back of the classroom, quite removed from the rest of the class. It was their niche, almost a club. Leaving them there enabled me to dub them "The Hole in the Wall Gang." Just hanging a slogan on the group was not my aim. It enabled me to identify the group as a group long before I knew their individual names. It also left them with a comfortable place to work and the beginnings of a group identity.

Decentralized communication. The reader should note that my groups have been from four to six persons. I shall add that each person typically has the same reading assignment before the group is assembled. Lecture chairs are moveable objects of furniture, enabling the group to sit in a circle. Thus each person has a common fund of data and no one has a position of prominence from the point of view of seating. Both these factors leave the group open to an exchange of views regarding the project assigned to the group. The group, then, is structured so that anyone can talk to anyone else with relative freedom. Why? Research has shown that decentralized communications networks in small groups are good for group morale and helpful for solving complex problems.[7]
I can say here that, having been given the reading assignment ahead of time, the group involves itself in the task of relating theory to practice, comparing different authors as well as mastering the assignment. In short, the problems assigned the group are complex. Morale among students taking required courses outside their major area of interest tends to be low. General studies courses fall into this category. Some of them are required for graduation. Student morale can certainly be an asset to learning, although of course the two do not exactly coincide. It is possible to be in good spirits at a circus while learning little. On the other hand, trying to teach a group of students who are discontented and discouraged cannot be viewed as a hopeful situation for any teacher.

2. Group Composition
Turning our attention to the individuals who make up

groups in the classroom, we find that empirical studies support the hypothesis that intelligent members are more active in a group and less conforming.[8] Furthermore, group members possessed of special skills related to the task of the group tend to be more active.[9] Within the classroom framework we can draw the rather simple conclusion that in the larger classroom framework, say a group of thirty, even the more intelligent members will be hindered in discussion by the sheer fact of numbers. I think of the analogy of a vegetable garden. The gardener must regretfully select the strongest plants. He must pull out the others, even strong plants. Given room, however, he may transplant the pulled up plants in another part of the garden where they will have a chance to flourish. I think it makes sense to transplant potentially active students to small groups where they will have more chance to take an active part in discussion. The same argument holds true for the participant having special skills germane to the problem to be solved.

I recall an otherwise reticent student of aeronautical engineering who suddenly surfaced in a small group that was analyzing a short story about the life of a sea gull. His knowledge of the science of flying provided criticism of the flight descriptions in the book and was useful to his group. In a larger group, I doubt that he would have surfaced.

Cohesiveness. Research supports the position that individual members who are positively oriented to other people have a great deal to do with small group cohesiveness and effectiveness.[10] It would be difficult, if not impossible, for a teacher to sprinkle each small group with friendly outgoing individuals. It's not so much that they are not there. The simple fact is that the conditions under which I teach conspire to bring me each semester a group of students who are largely unknown to me and usually unknown to each other. I set up exercises in the initial days of the course designed to break the ice between the students.[11] Although I am a part of this breaking of the ice, the primary intent is for the students to get a start on knowing each other. Initially, for the most part, the class will get to know each other on a basis of personal attraction. When it comes to form groups, I leave them free to form their own, thus quietly maneuvering them into situations where there is a good likelihood of their forming groups based on individual attractiveness. The assumption, of course, is that we have enhanced the chances of group effectiveness in tasks and that there will likely be some members in each group who are socially attractive and sensitive.

Another aspect worthy of note in the study of small groups is the composition of the assembled group. It is not hard to see that four or five individuals engaged in interaction with each other will provide what one might call the cake effect. A cake, after all, is more than the sum of some eggs, flour, shortening, and other ingredients. The blend of ingredients produces something more than the properties of the ingredients themselves. A group is more than the sum of the individual characteristics of its members. For example, a group that is characterized by high cohesiveness is also characterized by a high degree of communication between its members, considerable influence of the members on one another, as well as effectiveness in task accomplishment. Members tend to be satisfied and happy in the group.[12] High cohesiveness can be defined as regards groups much the same way one would describe a wad of bubble gum. You can pull it, you can stretch it, you can chew it; but it's hard to break. Highly cohesive groups are characterized by sticking together. The members stick to their group.

I offer some observations concerning highly cohesive groups in the classroom. If the research notes that such groups are effective in completing their task, it does not specify the task. The task might well be something other than the project assigned by the teacher. Bob and Carol and Ted and Alice may really dig their group, but what they have in mind might well be a discussion of a party at Bob's pad that night. They will get the assigned project out of the way as quickly as possible and then get on with the serious project, the party.

The high degree of social influence of the group upon individual members can be of real use in getting a group into a project. I recall, for example, despairing over four high school students. As individuals I could get no work from them whatever. All were good friends. When it came time to form a group, they immediately joined on the basis of their friendship. No miracles were performed in their group projects, but they did work at them. My attention was drawn to the fact that they immediately gave themselves a nickname as a group—The Wolf Gang. I also noticed that they parcelled out the reading so that at each meeting at least one of them would be prepared to tell the others what was in the reading assignment. When Ken skipped school the day he was supposed to be the chief information officer, the others were visibly angered. Ken, a habitual truant, was present on "his day" most of the time thereafter. Lectures from me meant nothing. The pride of the group was much more effective in getting him to school. A discerning teacher who observes a group which is truly cohesive would do well to let the group know that he or she has observed this quality in the group. It would be wise to encourage the group by way of pointing out to them that they have the potential of doing good work. Granted, the teacher may have to work at getting the agenda closer to the goals intended by the teacher rather than some disparate goals set by the group. I myself almost never try to break up such a group. I steer it, for it is a potentially valuable learning instrument.

Member diversity. Research has also shown that groups having within themselves individuals of diverse abilities and diverse personality profiles tend to be effective and satisfied.[13] I merely note here that students in a large university taking courses required across the board for all undergraduates, regardless of academic program, have a bewildering array of interests, abilities, and cultural backgrounds. One does not have to arrange this. It is here. The question is only to recognize it as a plus and to capitalize on it.

3. The Structure of the Group

Every group develops a structure: a pecking order, roles to be played, positions of power, norms to be followed, leaders. People of status within a small group tend to conform to

41

group norms but are given a certain amount of leeway to violate the norms.[14] It is difficult to determine who will have status in a small group. I have noticed on the part of students a certain respect for older students in class. A local banker, coming back to school in his forties, not only was cooperative in the classroom, but his fellow students gave him a certain leeway in discussion and felt no resentment if he missed classes. I note that as class leaders older people can be extremely useful because of their status. Generally, they can be counted on to go along with a project that might frighten or antagonize other students initially. It is a fairly simple strategy, when getting groups started on a project, to begin with those who can be counted on to conform. As their number builds up, it becomes more difficult for the reluctant students to stay out of the project. It becomes the norm to get in rather than stay out. Once it is established in the group that the majority of the members are willing to tackle a project, doing the project becomes a norm or rule for the group. One who consistently deviates from the norm will be pressured by the group to conform. Continued deviancy will likely result in the deviant being expelled by the group.[15] I recall a group of students who had agreed to work at analyzing psycho-sociological factors at work in religious celebrations. One of their members was a rather impassioned member of a small Christian sect. He seized the opportunity to seek to evangelize the other members of the group. This was not the task they had agreed on. The other members tried a number of strategies to bring him round to the work at hand. "Well, you may have something there, John, but about this project" gradually turned into some rather tart comments—"Damn it, John, we're trying to get something done. Quit interrupting!" John managed to disrupt the group sufficiently to prevent a thorough analysis. Their project was in turn given a grade of "C" by me. John then switched to another group and was much more cooperative with them than he had been in his first group. I note that no intervention was necessary on my part, except for the feedback provided by my evaluation of their work.

I should add that, hopefully, in any class, the teacher has the optimum chance for being the leader of the class. Such a position of leadership must be earned, however, as well as being bestowed from on high. Research in our area shows that a task-oriented leader is more effective when the group task situation is either very favorable or very unfavorable for the leader. On the other hand a relationship-oriented leader is more effective when the group-task is only moderately favorable or unfavorable for the leader.[16]

Although I rarely attempt membership in small groups as teacher, still, in presiding over a series of small groups and the class as a whole, the above hypothesis is useful for me as a teacher. Very often the initial sessions of General Studies courses could be described as very unfavorable for the teacher. I find it useful here to be very task-oriented.

"Here is the book list; here are all the assignments for the semester; we will have a test or project on each day's assignment and a project to be done before the semester is over." This is a no-nonsense, non-negotiable set of directions to the students. It is not delivered with venom but enthusiasm. It is firm, directive, and aimed at the task. Once we get into group work, it is likely that the situation will be moderately good or moderately bad, so I assume a different stance— friendly, non-directive, a resource person, a helper. I trust that as the semester draws to a close, enthusiasm gradually will have built up; we have a good situation. The ending of the course is a demanding project. Here I find it suits me well to be quite clear that I will be expecting first-class projects of well-defined dimensions. Task orientation again becomes the focus. The point of these remarks is not so much to erect a paradigm of leadership style in the classroom. Rather it is to show that, given one's own personal makeup, how one leads a class group depends on what is going on in the class. The situation in the classroom must be continually under review by the teacher. The more different the styles of leadership he has to suit each situation, the greater his chances are for helping the class have a profitable learning situation. Although the empirical work done on leadership in small groups has for the most part been done for groups smaller in size than the classes I teach, still the conclusions of such research can be fruitful ground for experimentation in leadership techniques.

4. Tasks and Goals

It is a truism that undergraduates assemble to take required courses for a wide variety of reasons. For many of them, such courses are only hurdles to be disposed of with as little pain as possible as one gets on with the more interesting work of one's major area. It goes without saying that unless the teacher comes up with a goal for the class that seems at least potentially of interest to the group, there will be minimum activity on the part of the class. In working with small groups in the classroom, the group will never really become more than a collection of bodies unless there is a goal of interest to the group.[17] An initial clarification of the goal must be understood, as well as how the paths leading to the attainment of that goal do affect the motivation of small groups as well as their efficiency in the tasks designed to reach the goal.[18] If I am contemplating teaching an undergraduate course in psychology, I would do well to choose a thinker concerned with youth. I have found success teaching the psycho-analytical theory of Erik Erikson, using his book *Identity, Youth, and Crisis.*[19] The book is difficult and scholarly. It pro-vides a good exposition of Erikson's stance as a psychoanalyst. Most important, however, it does so within the framework of contemporary youth's search for identity. Most of my students are young. Many of the older students are concerned with young people. The subject matter of the book lends itself to motivation for learning. I must further make it clear that peripheral readings are paths to the insights of Erikson. If I use J. D. Salinger's *Catcher in the Rye,*[20] it must be clear that the character of Holden Caulfield is related to Erikson's theory. Exercises in groups relating the one book to the other must sur-face as not mere exercises in analysis, but also as relating to the lives of the group members. If I am clear on the goal, and if my goal coincides with a touchpoint of interest on the part of

44

individual group members, the odds go up that they will tackle tasks with greater motivation and greater efficiency.

The long-term goal of the course, as well as the short-term goals, needs to be geared to success on the part of the students. Small group research shows that upon the successful completion of a task, groups generally aspire to tackle a more difficult task.[21] For this reason my early assignments and tasks for groups are calculatedly easier than later ones. They need to succeed a little bit. A group can catch the bug of success; I want to infect them a bit initially. The old proverb is here apropos: "Nothing succeeds like success." It's like a little boy deciding to be a professional fighter after licking the seven-year-old bully on the block.

I find it interesting to note that there is a well-established hypothesis concerning small groups, that a difficult task brings with it more frequent attempts at leadership among group members. Towards the middle of a course I gave my groups a difficult two-hour class assignment demanding a group report defining each of Erikson's eight stages of man, a motto for each one, a contemporary example from real life, and an example from a novel we had read for each of the stages. A quiet but intelligent fellow named Russ Smith suddenly emerged as leader in one of the groups. He had not attempted leadership in the group before, but realized that the job to be done really demanded his own thorough grasp of the matter. His understanding of the matter, his ability to synthesize, and to direct the group's comments had remained unnoticed by the group until a task of a really demanding nature was presented. At the end of the semester several of his group members remarked on his sudden emergence as a useful leader and expressed surprise that he had remained content to play a minor role up until that particular point in time. A student of small group behavior would have predicted the emergence of several Russ Smiths with the assignment of a difficult task. I was gratified, for the group learned a lot under Russ' leadership, as did he himself. It was not a chance emergence.

I find it useful that small groups engaged in difficult tasks tend to perform better if the members of the group can freely express feelings of satisfaction or dissatisfaction with the group's progress.[22] To stifle such expression would be detrimental to the group's efficiency. For this reason I attempt as a teacher to avoid what might be called the Watergate Effect. I don't want them to think that I hear everything that is going on in the group, lest my presence inhibit them. The very formation of a series of small groups in a classroom makes this nearly impossible in any event. Further, I instruct groups frequently to express dissatisfaction or approval, pointing out to them that it is not counterproductive. In point of fact, it helps.

In concluding our remarks about task difficulty, it seems important to note that research supports the notion that task difficulty is related to originality of solution in groups.[23] Related to this is what small group researchers call the "risky shift" phenomenon.[24] Many teachers have made use of groups on the assumption that a group of students would afford a system of checks and balances in making an analysis or solving a problem. The conclusion would likely be well worked out but neither original nor risk involving. My own work in the classroom supports both originality and risk in the solutions of group tasks. I'm thinking of a group who were assigned the task of making a collage, illustrating by pictures the classic stages of human development according to Sigmund Freud— oral, anal, and phallic. A middle-aged banker, an art student and two others put together three posters in a forty-five minute period—not just the one I called for. Each poster was shaped in contour like the appropriate organ in the theory—a mouth, an anus, and a penis. Photographs from picture magazines filled in the outline with typical behavioral scenes that had expressions of the three stages. Note that I called for only one poster and provided backing for the pasting that was oblong. The group knew that the posters would be mounted on the classroom walls. Their series of three was not only original, but demanded careful analysis of Freudian theory, and an expression of it using a medium with which only one of them was at all familiar. The collage was not only arresting to the eye but also a bit risque as decoration for the walls on a college classroom. This experience provides an illustration of both originality theory and the risky shift phenomenon. Other groups working on analysis papers have deliberately twisted the instructions of the project to suit their own curiosity and inventiveness. Groups have point-blank refused to turn in projects at the end of the allotted time, when their work seemed not quite satisfactory to them. They often fight my own evaluation of group projects. I note these small illustrations of group theory, not in the interest of solid empirical backing for the theory, but to show that these theories have been a fruitful ground of experimentation for me as a teacher. I am often surprised by both the originality and the involvement of these groups. Some degree of revolutionary activity on the group's part with regard to my instructions for projects seems fruitful. As an educator I am not really interested in rigid conformity to my own ideas, but originality and intellectual probing on the part of my students.

A few remarks on the time element in group projects. Studies have been done indicating that if one increases the difficulty of a task and at the same time demands rapid reaction time, a group tends to respond more effectively.[25] So, for example, if I give a difficult task to my groups and noticeably shorten the time they expected to have to complete it, they generally cut the small talk and get cracking. Many times in my career as a teacher I have had individual students complain that they did not have time to complete an assignment. It is truly educational for a teacher to find out what they actually can do when their backs are to the wall, the work is hard, and the time is limited. Often both teacher and students are surprised at the results.

On the other side of the coin, a task that requires a lot of cooperation on the part of group members tends to take longer than a project not requiring extensive interplay among the workers.[26] I only want to point out here that a teacher must be careful to assess the task assigned. A complex one may require considerable discussion by the group. To assign a very short time for such a project would likely stifle discussion and lead

47

to poor quality work as well as frustration on the part of the students. I find no easy rule of thumb for assigning time, except that a definite amount of time should be assigned; careful but unobtrusive observance of how the groups are doing can lead to a feel for how long a given assignment should take. On the spot extensions of the time limit seem sensible, if the situation calls for it.

C. Conclusion

At this juncture, the reader might well be thinking of a paraphrase of an initial quote in this essay, "Most teachers who write about teaching, write too goddamned much!" And so we have come full circle. I shall thus attempt a conclusion. I have presented the teacher who uses groups in the classroom as a possible antidote to the so-called "successful teacher"—the charismatic pied piper, or perhaps even the coercive "kick their asses" type. I further have some hope that the use of groups can be a corrective for the teacher who "talks too goddamned much."

It has been my concern, however, not merely to avoid pitfalls. This paper has been built on the work of social psychologists whose work has led them to hypothesize that "groups usually produce more and better solutions to problems than do individuals working alone,"[27] or the even more blunt statement "groups learn faster than individuals."[28] I quote these conclusions with full knowledge that there are many kinds of learning—as well as many kinds of groups. Group efforts at musical composition or the construction of English prose have generally proved unsuccessful. I can't avoid noting, however, that much early and contemporary jazz has been created by musicians while playing in ensemble. Nor can one pass over that fact that the great prose of the King James Version of the Bible was produced by a group.

The examples above only serve to show that a careful analysis of the task should be attempted before putting a group to work on it. We have attempted some suggestions indicated in the research on how groups should be used in the classroom. Task analysis, group structure, group composition and the physical environment of the group have been the headings under which we have made our comments and suggestions.

The fact that most of our references have been to a single book is not by chance either. The book is a summary of hundreds of studies of small group behavior. It is hoped that this one primary reference will lead the reader to check the references, possibly to read the book, and even to go on to further reading in this new but rapidly growing discipline—the study of small group behavior. This particular essay, it is hoped, will lead other teachers to use the dynamic of the small group as it fits their solutions and goals in the classroom.

CHAPTER III

ETHICAL ISSUES: AN ERIKSONIAN PERSPECTIVE

A. Eriksonian Psychology and the Golden Rule

The previous chapter was an essay on technique in undergraduate teaching. The present one concerns itself with the ethics of the student-teacher relationship.

The ancient formulation "Do unto others as you would have others do unto you" has merit in all human relationships. I wish here to apply it to the professor. The insights of Erik Erikson, used extensively in Chapter One, seem peculiarly apt to teaching.

We have previously noted that Erikson's pioneering work on a psychology of humankind is built upon eight unfolding stages of human life. This stage theory is at the heart of all his major work. It has peculiar relevance to ethical injunctions for the simple reason that it views people as growing while their lives continue. Erikson finds a different crisis at each of the stages he postulates from cradle to grave.[1] It is precisely the **difference** of each crisis from the others that leads to his preoccupation with ethical concerns.[2] His concern with what he calls fruitful patterns of interaction speaks directly to our concern in this chapter with the Golden Rule as it applies to teaching.

> Through the study of case-histories and of life-histories we psychoanalysts have begun to discern certain fateful and certain fruitful patterns of interaction in those most concrete categories (parent

51

and child, man and woman, **teacher and pupil**)
which carry the burden of maintenance from
generation to generation.[3]

The Golden Rule, as understood by Professor Erikson,
"would say that it is best to do to another what will strengthen
you even as it will strengthen him—that is, what will develop
his best potentials even as it develops your own."[4] It is best to
do what is needful for him or her to successfully weather his
crisis while it provides you with the resources for weathering
yours.

In any human interaction there is a difference of needs and
desires on the part of those interacting. Erikson's systematic
developmental look at human life enables one to see that, for
example, a middle-aged teacher does not ordinarily have the
same kind of overarching life crisis as the twenty-year-old
student with whom that teacher works. My concern here is to
explore the activities a teacher might employ to meet the
student's needs and thus enable him or her to deal successfully
with a person at a different stage in life. Were I to take the
Golden Rule statically instead of developmentally, I might
teach a twenty-year-old very poorly if I taught that student in
the manner that I myself would like to be taught. Erikson's
own musings about the authenticity of the college teacher
from the point of view of the student rebels of the 1960's
underscores the importance of seeing the difference between
college student and professor.[5] Bluntly put, the revolting
students of the late sixties had an acute need to know that their
profs were not phonies. They desperately looked for someone
worthy of trust. Contrast this with the attitude of older students, returning to college in mid-career. Both the Eriksonian
model and my own experience as a teacher attest to the fact
that the primary concern of the older students is whether the
professor does an adequate job in the classroom, so that they
can get on with the business of learning. The teacher's personal integrity is of less central interest to them than it is to
their younger classmates.

I do not wish here to make a long excursus into the causes of
learning, not to mention teaching itself, as a casual factor in

the learning process. Let me content myself with drawing a parallel between teacher and psychoanalyst and thus situate myself as a teacher before discussing the ethics of teaching. Erikson speaks of the psychoanalyst as

> ...helping the patient find out what can (and did) go wrong in his life, he must promote what in the patient's own nature is ready to heal itself.[6]

As a teacher I see myself as helping the student discover what she can (and did) learn in her life. I seek to promote what in the student's own nature is ready to learn by itself.

B. Transference and Countertransference

If one is to treat the ethics of the teacher in the light of doing unto others, it is important to see that the teacher may be subject to being "done to" or even "done in" by students in a manner at one and the same time natural (and therefore to be expected) and surprising. I refer to the phenomenon of transference:

> Transference is a universal tendency active in any relationship in which the other also "stands for" a person of the preadult past.[7]

The young man or woman may regard the authority figure of the teacher as one more parent, to be treated and resented as the real one was. Needless to say, a teacher may carry the burden of another punitive or resented teacher from the past of the student. It can be useful to recognize behavior in students under the heading of transference which could otherwise be shocking or unexplainable. They may not really be angry at you; it may be someone else. By the same token, if transference is possible from student to teacher, so is its reverse. It goes without saying that a teacher can invest students with characteristics of people in his or her own past.[8] In speaking of the clinician Erikson points clearly to the two edges of countertransference. It can be used to exploit the patient's transference and to dominate or serve, possess him or love him to the disadvantage of his true function.[9] It scarcely needs to be said that there is a parallel for teachers. To accept transfer from a student while refusing at the same time to exploit it is the challenge.[10] It is a challenge that speaks directly to the temptation, occupational in nature, to do one's student in, rather than to do unto them as you would have them do unto you. I think I can say with little hesitancy that as a teacher I am seldom seen as a person, for what I really am. Each of my students invests me with a number of people from the past. I hope not to trade on this investment. I hope not to exploit the weakness of the transference of my students. For I would wish that they would, from my teaching, grow in critical skills of my disciplinary or inter-disciplinary effort. I would hope that the shadows of the student's past will slowly recede in our relationship, and that one day I will be recognized for what I am, an individual and a teacher...neither God, nor lover, nor parent. Should I play God, parent, or lover to my students I should be abusing my position, taking advantage of theirs, not to mention impersonating a personage and taking a role that is not mine.

C. Particulars: The Identity Line

I do not wish to remain abstract in this discussion, a developmental treatment of human beings is precisely not static or abstract. I will then presume a concreteness for the teacher. I will presume that most undergraduate university professors are well into what Dr. Erikson refers to as the period of life characterized by a dialectical tension between generativity and stagnation.

If I do not choose to remain abstract in this discussion, be it also said that I do not wish here to repeat what I have already explored in Chapter One of this book. The celebrated eight stages of the life cycle are explained variously by Erikson himself.[11] They have been popularized ad nauseam.[12] It is my intent to jog the memory of the reader or to remind the reader once again to do a bit of investigation. To jog, then—Erikson sees each human being developing from birth through old age with an individual core both somatic and psychic. He or she must grow in a common culture, a world outside but constantly surrounding the individual. Each individual lives with and is marked by history, both a personal history and the history of the common culture. The ego is seen as an adaptive agency within the person, sorting out and screening the demands of outside environment, soma, and psyche.[13] The "job," if you will, of the ego varies as the person develops in a given environment. The entire life-span of the individual is seen as unfolding, growing, developing for good or ill in certain stages. Each stage has its own set of paramount polarities or pulls toward development or regression. Of these eight stages I am here concerned primarily with the stage of youth, the period between childhood and adulthood. Erikson sees it as a stage of extraordinary complexity and importance in the development of the individual. Each of the crises which preceded it resurfaces in a new way. Each of the crises which follow it presurfaces in this youthful recapitulation of all the crises of the life cycle.[14] Erikson sees this period of hopefully creative confusion as needing a period of moratorium or delay for sorting out and experimenting with the manifold complexities of youth.[15] This period precedes and prepares for some sort of central adult commitment which he sees as marking a human being deeply for the rest of the individual's life. I will let Erikson speak for himself of this central crisis.

> ...it occurs in that period of the life cycle when each youth must forge for himself some central perspective and direction, some working unity, out of the effective remnants of his childhood and the hopes of anticipated adulthood; he must detect some meaningful resemblance between what he has come to see in himself and what his sharpened awareness tells him others judge and expect him to be.[16]

It is my concern here to measure how a teacher of undergraduates can apply the Golden Rule to students living through this central crisis of identity. It is not too helpful to "do unto them as we would have them do unto us" or to "love them as we love ourselves" if, as George Bernard Shaw astutely pointed out, our tastes differ.[17]

Let us see if we can make an estimate of what their tastes are. We shall look systematically at the various aspects of this central crisis, that of youth, termed by Erikson the crisis of identity, to discover how the age-old rule might best be applied.

1. Temporal Perspective versus Time Confusion[18]

This aspect of identity crisis is related by Erikson to the first crisis of human life, the crisis of trust against mistrust, occuring in the first year of life.[19] Time confusion can be characterized by a deep distrust of time delay. Young people are often not patient with legitimate delays on the part of teachers, for example. They are likely to see a period of waiting as a personal betrayal, a time of seeming endlessness, interminable and insufferable. It is my feeling that a teacher must recognize this impatience for what it is—a struggle for trust that is nearly always present in youth, sometimes desperately so.

If I am to presume the professor to be older, to be fully embarked into adulthood, a word here is in order by way of description of the basic Eriksonian polarity of adulthood—generativity versus stagnation.[20] The term generativity is used in a broad sense. It deals with a period in life when one's central focus is the guidance of the next generation. Since our concern here is interaction between youth and mature adults, let me quote my guide where he contrasts them.

> From the point of view of development, I would say: In youth you find out what you care to do and who you care to be—even in changing roles. In young adulthood you learn whom you care to be with—at work and in private life, not only exchanging intimacies, but sharing intimacy. In adulthood, however, you learn to know what and whom you can take care of.[21]

Where the enrichment of caring does not take place, one finds a regression to a kind of intimacy, or the search for it, that is basically sterile and stagnant. My concern here is that the function of adulthood closely parallels the function of teacher. Indeed, one may say that the one is an aspect of the other. Adult care, generativity, guidance of the next genera-

56

tion are terms which demand that an adult be a teacher whether or not a particular person is a member of the teaching profession. Put another way, a professional teacher who is not an adult may well be a menace to students. The teacher who is on the prowl for intimacy from students is a great deal different from one who enjoys a real mutuality in the teaching relationship. Mutuality is the heart of any relationship between people. There is nothing unhealthy about a relationship in which partners depend on each other for the development of their respective strengths.[22] A teacher, then, who does not learn from and in some sense delight in his or her students is as sorry a spectacle as a student who neither learns from nor delights in teachers. I should hope that intimacy needs would be met in other relationships, for such relationships of intimacy between student and teacher strike me as inevitably a betrayal of the role of the teacher visited on a person very likely deeply searching for authenticity. Authenticity on the part of the teacher seems a key to trust in the teacher, regardless of one's approach to teaching matter. It is not permissiveness or strictness that is the issue. It is the credibility of either one as authentic.[23] Put another way, a teacher of youth must be worthy of the demands of their faith. Such a one, possessed of a rock-bottom honesty, can be instrumental in imparting knowledge; but more than this, this teacher, like every adult, is one who "takes care." Such a teacher is a healer, a promoter of the ability in youth to trust.[24]

2. Self-Certainty versus Self-Consciousness[25]

The crisis between autonomy and shame and doubt, characteristic of one- and two-year-old children,[26] surfaces in a new way in youth. The presence of the student uniform, whether old-style tie or skirt, whether new-style denim or corduroy, shows the protective coloring of the student. The protective coloring of blue or brown is useful for covering a multitude of uncertainties. How useful for a student to be branded a student while getting on with what he or she really is. If you're not too certain who you are, denim or corduroy can be a marvelous cover. From the point of view of the teacher it seems obvious to me that public stripping of that cover can be damaging to the student. I can think of ridicule and sarcasm in the forum of the classroom as in no sense promoters of self-certainty in the large sense, even though such punitive measure might bring about some grudging (and likely confused) work on the part of the student. An old teacher once told me, "Francis, never embarrass a boy." I can think of no clearer exposition of a developmental application of the Golden Rule to the self-certainty facet of youth in the classroom. Taking positive perspective, the word "guide" comes to mind here[27] with all its overtones of respect and care in the process of encouraging and promoting learning.

3. Role Experimentation versus Role Fixation[28]

The childhood stage occuring at the end of the third year of life may be characterized by a crisis of initiative against guilt.[29] This intrusive, exploratory period of childhood, taken up with role anticipation, finds new expression in youth. Erikson sees it as important for experimenting, trying on various hats, different kinds of jobs, attitudes, life styles. I feel that the role of the teacher can be vital to experimentation. I am thinking here of a punitive disdainfulness for young students who are experimenting with clothing, work habits, sex roles, attitudes toward authority that differ from those of the classic self-made-person identity so much a part of many of us a generation older.[30] I think rather of the great value of the teasing militancy of one of the great teachers of our time, Mohandas Gandhi.[31] Gandhi was a tease. He once gave Jan Christian Smuts a pair of sandals. Gandhi had made the sandals while he was in jail on Smuts' orders; they were an excellent fit. The fact that Smuts returned them, well worn, twenty-five years later is evidence that Gandhi's gift to his jailer was a gesture well understood by that adversary. The gift was a symbol at once of Gandhi's message, a suggestion, "If the shoe fits wear it... in more ways than one." It was a humorous reminder, a barb, but a non-violent barb.[32] For a teacher to tease students' minds, to trap them into insights, to needle them about their cognitive and emotional assumptions, is to encourage the experimentation of roles without trying to force it. Such a stance is at one and the same time playful and encouraging to those who would be playful in their pursuit of knowledge. Playfulness in the search for identity is as important as it is for children seeking to learn initiative and to come to terms with paralyzing oedipal guilt.[33] It is often in our games, our playfulness with life, that most serious experiments take place. Continued deadly earnestness on the part of teacher or student can be very deadly indeed, a death to curiosity, experimentation, the possibility of finding one's self.

4. Apprenticeship versus Work Paralysis[34]

Primary school children need very much to be able to make something work. Johnny needs to be able to read or play ball or do fractions.[35] His older sister or brother needs the similar experience of being an apprentice—the hard work, the satisfaction of coming to terms with a skill or a habit of thought, the competition inevitable in a demanding apprenticeship. I cannot but think of a description of a competition in drama won by a group of young people while actually institutionalized for emotional disorders.[36] In this case the drama group was organized primarily as therapy. How interesting that demanding schooling is therapeutic! How very possible for the teacher of college undergraduates in the name of leniency to be depriving students of the therapy of demanding cognitive growth. Such "leniency" can well be called sadism.[37]

5. Sexual Polarization versus Bisexual Confusion[38]

Sexual polarization does not so much look back at a stage of childhood as it anticipates a coming of intimacy of isolation.[39] It has to do with coming to grips with what kind of woman or man a person is, and is to be. It sets the stage for a style of intimacy to come later, or it can prepare for a life of isolation. I shall not reiterate my remarks made earlier in this chapter about the possibility of regression in an adult in the generative or "teaching" stage. I will not repeat here my reaction to the professor on the prowl for intimacy among students in the identity period of life. Suffice it here to say that when one's style of manhood or womanhood is appearing to one's self, one is especially vulnerable to being treated as no person at all, an "object" or target for pseudo-intimacy on the part of an older person.[40] To treat a person in search of his own sexuality as a thing is a lovely way to set the stage for that person's future isolation from others. A given teacher might well want to have "it" done to him or her; to assume the same from a student strikes me as perilous and perhaps perfidious.

6. Leader- and Followership versus Authority Confusion[41]

To follow well or to lead well is the question. To answer it is to set the stage for adulthood.[42] If the generative teacher is to help the student find that answer there is required of her or him, from both an Eriksonian and an ethical approach, the authenticity and mutuality before discussed in this article. I do not see the voice of the teacher as necessarily charming or overpowering. "Encouraging" is perhaps a good word, for it implies both respect for the student and a true mutuality or sharing between student and teacher. The parallel here between teacher and psychoanalyst is striking.[41] To see the teacher abdicating all other roles except that of the voice that encourages insight and helps with interpretation is a teaching role redolent with what one would expect from an adult, a truly generative person.

7. Ideological Commitment versus Confusion of Values[44]

Again, and lastly, we anticipate. Ideological commitment looks forward to the integrity of old age or its counterplayer, despair.[45] Since my professor does indeed use ideology as a characteristic of youth, at once necessary and transient, with implications for the Golden Rule, I shall let him speak:

> By ideology, in turn, I mean a system of commanding ideas held together to a varying degree more by totalistic logic and utopian conviction than by cognitive understanding or pragmatic experience. The ideological and moral orientations are, in turn, absorbed, but never quite replaced, by that ethical orientation which makes the difference between

adulthood and adolescence—"ethical" meaning a universal sense of values assented to with some insight and some responsible foresight.[46]

If, as the teacher, I am then to learn to expect my students to have invested their loyalty in simplistically overdefined ideologies, labelled by Erikson "totalistic,"[47] I am presented with a two-fold problem. First, I must not be surprised if in the give and take of classroom discussion they stubbornly adhere to a "message." I hasten to note that this message may well come under the guise of a cognitive system, learned in my own halls of learning. It can be behavioral psychology with a capital B, feminism with a capital F, black Americana studies with a capital B, to name a few. It is important that I see ideology in youth as part of their quest for truth. As such it needs to be tested by my student ideologues. As teacher I see here the value of testing and challenging "messages" without ridiculing them or those who hold them. If ideological orientation is a "total" orientation in young people, it is my job to see that those orientations are probed, lest my young people remain too long where they should be for a while, lest they or someone else be indeed "totalled" by this total orientation. My adherence to a developmentally understood Golden Rule as I teach totalistic youth seems not merely apt but ethical.

D. Conclusion

In terms of the teaching function I have discussed in developmental terms mutuality, authenticity, teacher as guide, teaching by teasing and playfulness, moral sadism, students vulnerable to being sex objects, the encouraging voice, and the challenge of youth's ideologies. I have attempted to focus on the ethical challenge of these phenomena. My specific ethical vantage point has been as enduring and ancient formulation for ethical behavior, the Golden Rule. My view has been born of Erikson's comment about Mohandas Ghandi's peculiar fusion of a non-violent religious tradition with political action.[48] In a small way, I have undertaken to take the heart of the Law and the Prophets in the Christian, Hebrew, and many other great religious traditions, and apply it in an Eriksonian developmental manner, to the teacher of college undergraduates. If occasionally the tone of these ethical musings smacks of moralizing, I can only say that my guide in this essay was acutely aware "that the loudest moralists have made deals with their own consciences."[49] It has not been my intention to "cast the first stone." It is my intention to cast some ethical light on my own profession.

I furthermore hope that if this chapter and the two that have preceded it have drifted inevitably towards abstraction, the chapter that comes next will be a corrective. A day-by-day account can provide a more enriching picture of the university as asylum, the use of small groups, the emergence of ethical problems in the classroom than a formal presentation might ever do.

With this hope I guide the reader to a portion of a teacher's journal.

CHAPTER IV

A TEACHER'S JOURNAL

A. Introduction: No Good Place to Start

The confused motorist stopped by the watermelon stand on a dusty back road in Eastern Kansas. The weather was July-drip. The sunny kind of drip, the kind where the only drip is trickling down from a wet slot on your shirt to where your belt bunches the shirt up on your hips. "How do you get to Topeka?" said the tourist. The reply from an old man in overalls, "If I was you, Mister, I sure as hell wouldn't start from here."

There isn't anyplace else to start, except from where you are, on a trip. So, I'm going to ask you to go with me on a trip through a part of a course entitled "Contemporary Theory and Human Growth." It's a General Studies Course at Western Michigan University. My notion is that many of us who are teaching interdisciplinary courses on the under-graduate level have the feeling that we always are starting at the wrong place.

I want very much to talk about my work, and so, wrong place or not, I'm just going to take you with me, hour by hour through a portion of this course. To do so for the whole course might be tedious. We will begin, then, at the start of the second of two main blocks of the course, centering around Erik Erikson's thoughts on Identity.

The goal of your trip? To understand what Erikson means by the word Identity and to use that notion to clarify an identity search on the part of the students, each one taken individually.

B. Taking the Trip
First Week

First class. It had to come, I know. Here we are in the middle of February. We've had fun so far in the course studying and sharing Viktor Frankl's will to meaning and seeing parallels to Frankl's ways for finding meaning in a rather roisterous novel by Clair Huffaker called *Nobody Loves a Drunken Indian*. But I know that the moment of truth has arrived, for Erikson's book on youth and identity is difficult reading. I don't know whether this class, taking the course to fulfill a General Studies requirement, will do the digging required to find what that wise old man has to say about youth. The first chapter of the book is assigned according to the sheet I have given them for reading throughout the semester. And so, I walk into Room 4510 Dunbar, a few minutes after one P.M. I often feel a tingle when I walk into class, reminiscent of the bell starting the initial round of a boxing match. No more planning or worrying, "You're on!"

I walk up to my desk, rummage through my brief case for last class's corrected test, my horrendously large sixty page, typed outline of Erikson's book, and my scribbled plans for today's class. Up to the board to write in my left-handed scrawl, two questions:

1. Does Erikson equate "crisis" with disaster? 2. Name one of the two conceptual ancestors of Erikson's notion of "Identity."

The answers are to be brief. During the five minutes they are pondering and writing, I prowl the classroom...there are some faces that are familiar, but the names? I take a fix on two or three faces—look down at the piece of paper on the lecture chair in front of them, and attempt to attach the name to the face. They are finished now, half-sheets of paper work their way to the front of the room where I gather them into a single stack. Looks like they have read the first chapter anyhow, except for Dennis Smith, who looks blank in his chair in the back

64

of the room. Does he have a book? Did the bookstore run out? Did he just decide, "The hell with it"?

We spent nearly the whole class sharing thoughts from two early writers on identity, both quoted by Erikson in the chapter. William James's letter to his wife I shall quote in part here:

> A man's character is discernible in the mental or moral attitude in which, when it came upon him, he felt himself most deeply and intensely active and alive. At such moments there is a voice inside which speaks and says: "THIS is the real me!"

It was a good session. The students were loose enough to share experiences parallel to James's. Britt Theuer, a musician, describes his experience of feeling really himself when he is playing the trumpet. I cajole, wait and comment. Picking up on the thread of James's thought I point out that this feeling or voice does not guarantee that Britt will be a great trumpet player, it is a feeling of active tension, a time when one is willing to take a risk. Often such a voice speaks within us when we least expect it. I remember my own experience when I first began to teach high school—something inside told me that this was where I belonged, in the classroom—and oh, the surprise of it! I did not expect to find myself there nor hear that voice. Teaching was a part of my training as a Jesuit, and so I went. Not everybody heard a voice that year in Kansas City, 1956.

And so we shared experiences—for nearly an hour and a half, students speaking, shyly, almost warily, many of them. When it seemed that we had run out of responses to James's description, we went on to Freud's comments on his debt to Judaism. I shall quote again:

> What bound me to Jewry was (I am ashamed to admit) neither faith nor national pride, for I have always been an unbeliever and was brought up without any religion though not without a respect for what are called "ethical" standards of civilization...there was a perception that it was to my Jewish nature alone that I owed two characteristics that had become indispensable to me in the difficult

course of my life. Because I was a Jew I found myself free from many prejudices which restricted others in the use of their intellect; and as a Jew I was prepared to join the Opposition, and to do without agreement with the "compact majority."

Again the shy testimonies. I remember Larry Bolton describing his own Jewishness in terms similar to Freud's. Somehow his affiliation with Jewry made him feel he did not need the agreement of the majority of his peers. He talked of his freedom from certain kinds of prejudice as a part of his heritage. Larry talked to me later about a family of Georgia rednecks whom he greatly admires—country folk, given to making generalizations about "niggers"—but Larry saw another side to them. Maybe it does help to be Jewish!

It's over now—a long class of an hour and fifty minutes with no breaks, but a good one. The time seemed to go fast and I didn't have to talk too much.

Second class. The assignment was Erikson's second chapter. It concerns the basic tasks of the ego—as a central organizing agency absorbing historical, biological, and social data for the individual person.

Given a short test on the meaning of ego, somehow the direction of sharing takes a historical bent. Pete Kane and Steve Francis both talk of the history of their time in Viet Nam. Both functioned well for their country as soldiers. Steve was, as he put it, "blown up"—I didn't realize how literal a term that is. He was leaning over a live hand grenade in the dark when it detonated. The point of both men—they were set to come home as heroes for their country—one a hospital case, the other a proud young man. Both were greeted by no one. They were organized to be heroes from their own personal histories at war. This "history" made it damned hard to adjust...to being just ordinary Joes in civilian life. As Pete said, "It was terribly confusing."

I talked briefly concerning Erikson's conviction that exploited people usually accept the image given them by their exploiters. There is a history of this—both personal and familiar among black people in our country. If people say that

66

black people are shiftless niggers for long enough the ego will organize this data as acceptable. I noticed the small minority of black students I have in class nodding their heads. They said nothing.

Sharing centered around family and school. If your teachers have always thought you were dumb and told you so, well, there is a good chance you will believe them. If your mother thinks your older brother is the smart one in the family, you'll probably believe her too. These are historical aspects in ego development. I'm intent on the class seeing this time element, a developing and dynamic way of looking at the ego.

After class Pam Colen quietly came up to me and said, "Mr. Gross, when you were explaining the class project that we have to do, you mentioned two of the best you ever got were not written—one a dance of some Eriksonian theory; the other a series of drawings of faces showing Erikson's developmental states. Did you say that the two best projects you ever got were done by black people?" I looked Pam in the eye, not remembering that I had said anything about race in connection with the projects. "That's right, Pam." That mixture of surprise and pleasure in a young woman's face was born of a history of hearing things differently. She should have taught the class.

Second Week

First class. I'm not going to teach today—just turn them loose tracing Erikson's eight stages of personhood—from cradle to grave. They've read[1] it, I hope. I'm not worried so much about working with groups anymore. Some of the shock of helping one another in a "test" is over. The group getting the same grade, each one for the test—they are used to that. I hope they are ready. The task: in an hour and forty minutes groups of four to six must define each stage; give an example of each, find Erikson's supporting institution, and his motto for each.

Off they go. I feel up tight with nothing to do at first. I start watching the groups. One group is into making up their own mottoes for each stage—not rebellion, just their style, what the group researchers call "risky shift."[2] This observation is a reminder for me to sit down, draw a map of the room with each group identified in it, and observe. The group at the far left close to my desk has a guy pulled way back from the others—he's not into the project. I note that. Another group of four right in front of me are pulled so close together in their lecture chairs they look like a four-leafed clover—something doing there. Way in the back I notice two women looking out the window vacantly. And so I work my observation round the room—and then start again. I remember that groups change—next observation has my guy who was pulled way back, in closer. Later I discover the smokers in his group were bothering him—it took a while but they needed him. The groups keep changing—I make my notes on my second mental tour, not actually hearing what they are saying, but watching seating, eyes, how loud they are talking, whether there are any laughs.

I'm off now—touring the room, one group at a time. I tell them what I have noticed. The noise level is high, not just a buzz. "Hey Frank!... Do we have this right?" or "Leave us alone, Frank, we've got a good thing going here." What was an orderly tour becomes me actively scooting around the room. I spend some time with groups who are lost—needling, questioning, waiting for them to tell me to get lost, because I'm using up their time.

Back to the desk and my class list—I know students more and more now by what group they tend to be in. It's interesting to see floaters. They are often the ones that don't come to class much or don't do the reading. They aren't too welcome, so they shift from group to group. It does put pressure on them to come and to read. Is that fair? I'm not sure. Suddenly the period is coming to a close. I tell them to type the papers and xerox a copy for each in the group...and they are gone.

Second class. They are back, most with xeroxed copies, so I go carefully through the whole exercise myself out loud. Students sit separately, making notes, groaning, questioning my way of looking at the eight stages, but they are paying attention—except for those poor souls who weren't here last

68

time. Somehow I feel sorry for them. It is possible to be sick or bored or just to be upset—and hence missing from an important class. Going over something students haven't done can make them feel even more out of it.

A brief test on the assigned reading for today. We are starting the *Catcher in the Rye*, so I suggest how Holden Caulfield's life might have gone, partly from the book we have started, partly from imagination, for *The Catcher* gives us only a few days in the life of a young man in an Identity crisis. That's why we are taking the book. I want the students to come up for air and enjoy the book, but to deepen as well what they have learned by watching, laughing, and crying with a young man from the vantage point of Erikson. I hope the novel will bring them a step closer to applying the theory to themselves.

Finishing touch—for the last fifteen minutes of the period we do a body sculpture of Holden. We push back the chairs, put everybody in the middle of the room standing close together. Then some volunteer arranges hands and bodies into a sculpture representing Holden. Marguerite, who has a son at Michigan State, arranges one fellow sitting in the middle, a ring of others making gestures of despair, another acts surely, slowly the group see what she is about—Holden's terrible loneliness combined with his inability to accept intimacy. Three or four other sculptors try their hands at it...but not with the care of Marguerite—she is thinking of her own son surely; it shows.

Third Week

First class. The middle section of *The Catcher*. I think they are enjoying the book. Somehow it doesn't bother me anymore that some may have read it before. My students for the most part have read very little. That's one of the reasons for my using novels—it's never too late to discover the fun and potential wisdom of a well written book.

We are looking forward to Erikson's treatment of Identity crisis now, but I don't tell the students. I put seven key words on the board, taken from the book, that nearly correspond to the key headings in Erikson's treatment and call for small groups to give examples. The words: any Salinger fan will recognize a few of them—phony, sex, student, Old Jesus, Old Spencer and history, "I really am." I'm leading up to Erikson's categories of time as allied to trust, sexual polarization, the importance of ideology, the need to follow or lead effectively, role experimenation, having a feeling of apprenticeship, the need for self-certainty.

Put in other terms: Holden has a desperate need to trust someone, but he has been betrayed often. Almost everyone is phony to him who has been betrayed. His preoccupation with his own sex and with homosexuals shows a yet unsettled feeling for what kind of male he is. As a student, he is locked into one role—that of a professional flunker. His deep feeling for Jesus reflects his idealism, indeed his ideology. His encounter with his history teacher, Spencer, shows his despair at doing anything well. The oft-repeated "I really am" implies that he really isn't sure of what you the reader really thinks of him. But I don't want to get all that clinical—I want students to find Holden as he is. If they do, likely enough they'll see something of themselves. We'll leave Erikson for later.

After putting the words on the blackboard, I ask each group to brainstorm for fifteen minutes. Write down any associations they may make between these words and the book. After this they can argue out which ones seem most apt to the words and episodes in this book.

It takes TIME! Suddenly there are only fifteen minutes of class time left. I had hoped to have them do picture-posters of Holden in groups, cutting out photos from magazines and pasting them, collage-like, on paper backing. Maybe next semester I'll be more organized. My black suitcase with magazines, rubber glue, scissors, backing and two-way tape for mounting the posters on the wall weighs fifty pounds! Back to the office with it—ugh!

Second class. We have finished reading the saga of Holden Caulfield, and so today I throw a chintzy, twenty question fill-in test, taken individually, at the class. I know they don't learn much from this sort of exercise. Why do it? I do need to know who is doing the work in the groups, those who are doing the reading. Something down deep in me tells me that this is only an excuse. Tests that are not learning exercises bother me. My next dilemma—after correcting it later I find that everybody got almost all of the answers right. Well, they ARE reading. That's good, I hope.

After the fifteen minutes for the test we spent an hour and a half running through all the crises of adolescence explained by my friend Erikson as they happen to Holden. I explained each one; the students in large group session picked out examples. They were lively! The time went quickly. What I do not know—will the whole damned thing stay a nice, neat exercise, carefully segregated from their lives? "Class, today's puzzle is how to make a freaky kid in a novel fit into a developmental psychoanalytical model about adolescent and young adult identity crisis." Source of Hope: I think they like Holden, many of them. Can "like" be a word close to "identify with"?

Fourth Week

In seventeenth century European Jesuit Colleges—Voltaire was a graduate of one of them—one always "prelected" the lesson. They still do that! I can't resist thinking that James Joyce and Fidel Castro graduated from Jesuit schools of a later date. You see, "prelecting" means teaching something before you assign it, but it may help understanding too. I have been prelecting the actual reading of Erikson's chapter on Identity Confusion by means of my wistful adolescent in his field of rye.

And so—to it. Both periods this week will be spent by the students working on that chapter I hope they have read. We have worked so hard on learning the rules of group consensus—what must they do?

1. Define in their own words each of the seven aspects of adolescent and young adult identity crisis.

2. Relate each one to its corresponding earlier or later crisis in life as seen in the book.

3. Give an example from the experience of one of the group members of each of the aspects.

4. Define the word "moratorium" as it is used by the author and give an example as in number 3.

71

I am back playing "Nancy Nurse," visiting groups, pulling back from them and observing how they are doing. When the period is over, if there has been confusion, maybe they will bone up on what they didn't understand for the next class meeting! For the next meeting will be more of the same.

So this week has been a group-project week. Somehow I want to describe the group that did, in my opinion, the best project. Pete Kane is twenty-five, has two children, and is the group humorist—only later do I find out that he is very widely read. Steve Francis, my serious ex-Special Services soldier with his battle scars, who has a gift for digesting the lively conversation of the group on paper. Rich Sharpe, who is younger, an intense young man who is competitive—he quit another group that wasn't working hard enough to suit him earlier in the semester. And Sue, who is very quiet, except when she disagrees with something—a discerning listener in her blue coveralls, not as noisy as the others, but not taking a back seat either. The work of their week has a clear, simply put grasp of the theory and concrete examples that smack of reality. They are proud of their work—they enjoy it too!

Fifth week

Somehow last week's work was like being on a canoe trip. Two people in a canoe in the water have only a few feet between them. A pair of canoes on a river often don't have much space between them either. Decisions have to be made, cooperation is necessary. It's fun, if you work together, but it's demanding and often irritating. We've been on the river for a week. It's time to get out of the water, feel a different surface, get a little distance from one another.

We will spend this week and part of next week reading an autobiography, *I Know Why the Caged Bird Sings* by Maya Angelou.

First Class. I give a short individual test and we're off talking about Maya's early life—a discussion involving the whole class as a unit. Maya is a black woman; her childhood involves living with three different units of an extended American Black family.

In the beginning the discussion is mostly by white

72

students—dismay at a child's being shuttled back and forth between different relatives in widely separated parts of the country. Obviously her childhood is a disaster. Fifteen minutes into the discussion Tim Montgomery, a young black man from Detroit, almost plaintively asks, "Doesn't anybody see anything good in her early life?" Tim explains that his own life was not totally different. He didn't know his father until he was twenty. He lived with a grandmother for a while, with different aunts and uncles at various times during his childhood—and doesn't feel deprived at all. He was always at home—felt the basic trust and recognition Erikson feels is so necessary for a child. He wasn't just a parcel being passed around. He was a person and his scattered family knew who he was.

Somehow the class gets firing back and forth at Tim. He explains. They question...best of all, I'm not saying much. That's hard on me, but good for the class. I talk too much anyhow. Slowly the conversation dies down. The four blacks in the class become silent. The rest of us are a little embarrassed, as I see it. Just before the period is over Ron Karlis explodes, "We haven't gotten this thing off the ground. How come all you guys are afraid to talk?" He's disgusted and angry.

The class drifts off, but Ron stays. Jeff Patton stays too, a thoughtful impish black man—and a few others. I hang around and a spirited rap session runs for a half hour; differences between blacks and whites. That was fun! I wonder what other class they missed. I didn't get to lunch, but it was worth it.

Second class. More of Maya. A black girl is raped when she is eight years old in St. Louis, Missouri. She is sent South by her family to live in a small town in Arkansas. It is there in the protective cocoon of a close black community that she begins to recover from the trauma of rape. Her small community understands pain; it is a part of their lives. In a one-room school she begins to live again as a precocious student. Kids just don't survive if they can't make something work—the healing power of learning. I recall my years working with il-

73

literate boys in a State Industrial School in Topeka, Kansas. Case history after case history revealed to me the terror and desperation born of being in primary school unable to read. One of the most effective therapists in that school was a well-trained teacher of remedial reading.

In class we talked about primary school teachers. How well those college kids remember the one teacher who helped them read or learn basic Math skills, who cared enough to help them if they weren't doing well. This is Erikson's fourth stage; industry versus inferiority.

I find myself wondering why those memories are so vivid of the helpful teacher. My students are at Erikson's Identity stage, most of them, when once again a sense of apprenticeship is often a glue that holds them together. I know they need the healing of being able to make something work here in college just as much as they did in grade school. That need revives a host of memories. The whole period went by discussing and remembering.

Sixth Week

First class. They have finished the autobiography. In groups we take Maya through the eight stages of life, from cradle to grave—some of it is in the book, most of her earliest life they must imagine, as well as her later life, for the book ends when she is sixteen years old. The groups find it hard to see how there can be consecutive periods in an individual's life with a crisis that is peculiar to each. The novel lends credence to the theory. Perhaps they are beginning to see.

Then we go through all the crises of Identity—the years of adolescence and young adulthood, seeking examples in Maya's life. We are closer to home now. Her impatience and sense of betrayal at any delay, her self-consciousness, her fighting the role of the traditional black, her confusion as to whether or not she was a lesbian, her need of encouragement not to be a blind follower of traditional black behavior, her cause—to be black and to be somebody with its accompanying sense of mission— they are all crowded so close together, so important and critical for later years.

What do I hope for? A slight opening on the part of white

74

students into one black woman's life, but much more than this. Maya's story is in a sense their own story. Her confusion their confusion. Her hope their hope. Maya Angelou is primarily a human being—and so are they.

Seventh Week

First Class. Back to our rhythm of out of the canoe and onto the less confining bank. We take Erikson's chapter on youth. It is an encouraging but confusing chapter. I teach the hell out of it. A lot has been pent up in me too after a week of low profile.

And so I characterize contemporary youth as shiftless and shifty. A feisty little Irish-American girl erupts at being called shifty—she's tired of being put down when she has worked so hard trying to find herself. I hold my tongue, let her finish. She had described so well what Erikson has observed; seemingly shiftless young people are often in search of something or someone worthy of trust. It is a hard search; one must begin over, and over, and over. My short female has taught well what I was going to teach.

And so I shift. Youth's need to be a special kind, to be unique, the counter-cultures of varying kinds. Such lovely goals, but so close to the intolerant arrogance of a master race, or as Erikson calls it, a "pseudo-species." Super races are destructive; for they have no use for lesser species of human beings. I warn them.

The fear of determinism—how well my students know they are headed for a well-programmed future in a technological society. They want to take their time before commitment— and so they should. Their reticence about making commitments of a lasting nature comes out in class. I agree—yes, wait...but don't forget that whatever lasting choice you eventually DO make will indeed be made of the stuff of your past. You can't change your past, I tell them, you can only work with it. I am accused of preaching. That's fun for I can blow up with no wholly feigned anger and ask them what the hell do they expect from a teacher who spent twenty years studying and practicing the art of being a preacher. I can't leave my past behind any more than they can, damn it! I can only work with it.

There is more in this long class lecture, but this is enough for flavor.

The second part of the period is spent in groups. I give each group an overhead transparency sheet and three different colored felt pens. Their task—to define search for something worthy of fidelity and to draw a symbol of what this means. Each group will have the chance to flash their transparency and explain to the others what it means.

Second Class. Womanhood and inner space.

Well, I knew this one was going to be a crunch. The reason? It's two-fold. My own history from the time I was a little boy has been one of causes. I won't go into detail, but there was an identity crisis in my life too. It was slowly and irrevocably solved by my joining the Jesuit Order long ago and finding my place in that organization by being a teacher-preacher-priest. Just because I am not formally affiliated with the Society of Jesus anymore doesn't mean that bent for taking up social causes in the classroom has left me. Erikson would chuckle, no doubt, that I am in the third generation of four generations of American born Catholic priests.

To some extent perhaps that's why I find my most interesting students to be female and/or black. Many of my girls, many of the small number of black students who find their way into my classes, are bent on finding a new identity. They are serious, often confused, but their struggle has a quality that speaks to me.

Erikson's chapter on womanhood is not popular with my female students who are involved in the liberation of females in general, themselves in particular. If I understand correctly, it is because one of the cardinal tenets of what they call "the movement" is that women differ from men mainly for cultural reasons. Erikson's insistence that anatomy, in this case the female anatomy, is a major factor in one's identity, my girls flatly deny. It is true that Erikson uses his "anatomy is destiny" theory as a call for women to take their place with males in the public arena as equals. He feels the ground plan of a woman's anatomy gives her a certain inner quality, a concern with inner productivity rather than outer exploitation—the male syndrome of industrial production for its own sake, outer exploitation, war, exploitation of nature. The old calypso tune, "Man smart, woman smarter," is his theme...based on the ground plan of anatomy.

I am content to run a rather sloppy class juxtaposing Erikson with current thinkers who take issue with him. Often it is lively, because there are such strong feelings. We carry on with numerous digressions for an hour.

Somewhere, in an off moment, a young man with a frown on his face hesitantly raises a hand. We are approaching the end of the year, he notes. We do not have an examination but a paper or project, but the handout I gave them at the beginning of the year said something called an "interface paper" would be due a week before the semester ends. It's getting to be close to that time. Would I explain it?

My explanation and rationale went something like this.

"We have done a lot of reading in this course. I am not so much concerned that you master all of the reading in such a way as to be able to render it up, like the coin of tribute, at the end of the semester. My hope is that somewhere in this course, something has intrigued or troubled you as a student. I am not referring to peripheral things, but rather to something central in the thought of the two main thinkers we have taken— Viktor Frankl (the earliest portion of the course not dealt within these notes) and Erik Erikson. What I am looking for is a careful second look on your part at that thing that intrigued or troubled you, a careful analysis of it in your own language. That would be a book report, but I want more than a book report. I want you to bring your own experience directly to bear on that idea or series of ideas. I want you to recall, if you can, just why and how that idea touched your experience of life. A simple recalling of your experience can be called a journal. This is a journal of a particular sort. It is a journal of how that book affected you, what it reminded you of in your life, how it spoke to you. I do not want outside references and footnotes. I want you to tackle that idea, the same way a football player tackles another football player holding the ball. I want a collision. A possible title might be "How I Collided with Identity."

I ask myself why I want this. It is simply because I see little use in knowing something that doesn't somehow speak to my own experience. Three years of working with interface has led me to conclude that the wasted energy of getting somebody else to do one's term paper seldom occurs here. By and large one's feelings tend to be sacred.

In passing I note that the written medium for interface is most usual, but that some students may be more at home with another medium. I have received water color sketches of Erikson's eight stages, I have had students of dance work them into dance form. They have appeared in poetry, sculpture and photographs. I ask only that if they decide on a medium other than prose, that they check it out with me beforehand. In point of fact my most memorable interfaces have come in another form than the standard six typewritten pages. If there is a way to measure whether or not the goals of my course have been met, I find this kind of interface a most valuable tool, for it tells me not only whether or not my students have been able to undersand what we have discussed, symbolized, and read. I could do that, very likely with a standardized test. My goals include whether and how they were moved by that understanding.

Eighth Week

First Class. Once a semester I do it—a movie. This one is "The Autobiography of Miss Jane Pittman." It is a long and painful film of development. A child who is a slave travels through time, living the history of her part of Southern United States, culminating as a hundred-and-ten-year-old civil rights activist in the sixties. The tension, the pain, the search for fidelity—something or someone to be true to. I hope it sums up or dramatizes much of what we have been about this semester.

As the film opens I stand outside the theater and pick up the interface papers and sundry objects—everything from third-rate collages to sculptures, to developmental poems. I have four days to correct and scrutinize about a hundred of them.

They are more fun to work with than a hundred examinations, that much at least.

Second Class. Erikson's last chapter focusing on race and the wider identity. I pull out all the stops in the old mouth organ and teach, old-fashioned style, like crazy.

The word "Identity" is prominent in contemporary black literature, usually an agonizing negative identity attempting to find itself in a compact majority that simply does not see its name, to paraphrase James Baldwin. The history of the American black people strikes me as being a dark glass through which all young adults can see themselves—nameless, faceless, shiftless—searching, searching, searching.

I talk of the dilemma of integration, which so often means absorption or submission. The segregated campus here at Western Michigan University is not by chance, nor do most of us who are white have much understanding of it. And yet my great-grandfather's family were segregated too. They were immigrants, finding a place in another country—again I think of the title of a book by Baldwin. They were forging a new identity. Not surprising that they stuck together in church, marriage, school, and play—just to survive! Black people have been in my country longer than most of my own Catholic people, but they have been denied a positive identity. They stick together here at school just as my forebears did. Why should we expect them to be like us, who have robbed them of much of what is positive in their identity?

I lecture, knowingly talking to white students, of what a mind-blower it must be to discover the joy of being black. A black student throws in what a real mind-blower it was for him to discover a positive kind of black consciousness here at Western, a real revolution in consciousness. I talk of this of Erikson's hope that neither blacks nor whites will remain racists, for there is, in the last analysis, but one race. His fear, repeatedly expressed, of a super race, white or black. One must discover the human race in one's identity just as importantly as one discovers the beauty of being black.

Ninth Week

A hundred interfaces have each a short paragraph from me

79

now and a grade. I have averaged those grades into those of the daily quizzes, counting the interfaces a third of the mark. So many students I knew only vaguely before have surfaced as real people in those interfaces. A feeling of frustration wells up in me, for as things are coming to a close I feel a closeness to many of those people, now, for the first time.

The walk to class with stacks of papers and odd-shaped packages containing posters, sculptures. There is a single slip of paper containing the initials of each student in alphabetical order with the final grade recorded next to each student's initials.

Most of them are there in the classroom when I get there, so the paper with the final grades is passed around the room while I call out the names on the projects from each one to pick up his or her interface. It is a time of intensity.

Now we form a circle of chairs, putting me in the middle, and I ask each student to give me a letter grade for the course, outloud, with a short verbal editorial if they choose to make one. I want to do this; somehow it seems fair that I get the same form of grade the university requires me to give them. Slowly, around the circle each student speaks. It is purging but uncomfortable, but a good time to speak, for I have given them all the data I can—the emotions are as real now as they ever will be. Some rake me over the coals for not explaining the matter enough. Others say it was too difficult. Still others found real personal help. My grades vary from A to D.

The circle is completed. Most of them leave. Perhaps ten stay—some close to tears, some waiting to say goodbye. Again we sit in a circle. I explain that we will each initially give a sentence beginning with the words "I think." After all have said this, we will go around again beginning with "I see." After all have filled that sentence we will begin with "I feel." Then, looking directly at someone in the group, "I think you feel." The last sentence begins, "I want to tell you."

It is a progression game, increasing in intensity with each round. By the time we are finished several of my good people are in tears, but the reasons for their stay after the others were gone is apparent—gratefulness or resentment for a grade or some aspect of the course. I remember Steve telling one of the girls who had worked very hard on a series of pictures which I judged not to show Erikson's theory, how ten years go he had flunked out of school. Pete tells her not to pay too much attention to teachers. If she is proud of her work, that's enough.

One grade is a simple error on my part. I change it. The others remain the same. At least I have confronted them all face to face.

I feel a little beat up. My grades were sometimes as difficult to take as theirs were. Anita said, "Frank, you're a good guy, but I didn't get anything out of the course." It has been blunt, but I like that. I know I'm a good teacher, but it's hard not to be super, because, always I want to be better—and to be liked too.

And so they are gone. Most of them I will not see again. Will I ever hear of a lyric poet named Sharon White or a talented cartoonist named Jeff Patton? I hope so.

CHAPTER V

INTELLECTUAL DEVELOPMENT IN THE UNDERGRADUATE: ERIKSON AND PERRY

A. Introducing Perry and Erikson

This chapter is concerned with understanding the thought process of college undergraduates. It returns the reader to a treatment of the educative process. More formal and less narrative than the preceding chapter, it purports to be of help to those engaged in teaching undergraduates. The scope is restricted to the work of William G. Perry, Jr. and the now familiar Erik H. Erikson. I wish to compare, contrast, and to synthesize the work of these two theorists in so far as they describe the thinking processes of the young adult in college.

Both Erikson and Perry were at Harvard University for the full decade of the nineteen-sixties. Both are psychologists. Both developmentalists. Perry's work concerns itself with intellectual development among college undergraduates.[1] Erikson's concerns as a psychoanalyst obviously are too broad to list here. My concern in this chapter has to do with Erikson's position as the founder of a psychology of identity and crisis among youth.[2]

B. Perry's "Commitment" and Erikson's "Identity"

Erik Erikson is not at all backward in seeing a simplistic world view as a necessity for people who have left childhood behind and are searching for adulthood.

...at no other time does he so need oversystematized

thought and overvalued words to give a semblance
of order to his inner world.[3]

Erikson sees indoctrination from a benign, even an approv-
ing stance when mapping the path to identity for youth.[4]
Youth simply needs such a world view in order to maintain a
trusting view of the world. A view of the world that is well formulated, and of necessity simpler than the world itself, is a
powerful tool in the maturation process. It is only by living an
ideology that one can find how much it is worth a mature investment.[5] Indeed, Erikson characterizes youth as a time of
seeking something worthy of fidelity.[6] The quest must begin
somewhere, and beginnings are generally more simple than
endings.

What concerns and intrigues me here is the parallel between
what Erikson means by ideology and what William Perry
means by dualistic thinking.

> Dualism or Duality: A bifurcated structuring of
> the world between Good and Bad, Right and
> Wrong, We and Others.[7]

If I do not miss the mark, we can say that Erikson's ideology
is a world view that is characterized by dualism in Perry's
sense. Perry's ten-year study of Harvard and Radcliffe
undergraduates found most first-year students somewhere on
a scale of dualistic thinking.[8] By the time students were seniors
75% of them had "advanced" from dualistic thinking to a
more contextual and relativistic kind of thought, and beyond
this to a form of commitment.[9] Perry defines Relativism as
follows:

> A plurality of points of view, interpretations,
> frames of reference, value systems and contingencies
> in which the structural properties of contexts and
> forms allow of various sorts of analysis, comparison
> and evaluation in Multiplicity.[10]

His Harvard study gives us a picture of students arriving at
Cambridge with a simplistic way of thinking. There, they are
confronted by an educative process calculated to help them see
that all disciplinary knowledge is contextual and situational,
that a good answer is always tentative, never absolute. Most of

the students slowly make such a point-of-view their own. Only after such a switch in thinking processes do they, as indicated above, take a further step in their style of thinking.

Perry labels this new thought process "Commitment":

> An affirmation of personal values of choice in Relativism. A conscious act or realization of identity in responsibility. A process of orientation of self in a relative world.[11]

The "Commitments" discovered in Perry's interviews varied widely in object and intent, from career decisions to personal commitments such as marriage. It is important to see that these commitments are made within the context of relativism; they do not have the simplistic stance of the dualist. Relativistic thinking alone, Perry points out, cannot narrow itself to commitment to any one thing. By its nature it allows a myriad of answers to any intellectual problem of worth. Its very sophistication does not allow one to settle on any one answer. Commitment, however, involves a leap of faith. It involves taking responsibility; it involves identity. I think it is germane to my comparison here to quote William James as selected by Erik Erikson in a description of what Erikson means by identity. I want the reader to see the parallel between identity and committed thinking.

> A man's character is discernible in the mental or moral attitude in which, when it came upon him, he felt himself most deeply and intensely active and alive. At such moments there is a voice inside which speaks and says: "This is the real me!"

Such experience always includes

> ...an element of active tension, of holding my own, as it were, and trusting outward things to perform their part so as to make it a full harmony, but without any **guaranty** that they will. Make it a guaranty...and the attitude immediately becomes to my consciousness stagnant and stingless: Take away the guaranty and I feel...a sort of deep enthusiastic bliss, of bitter willingness to do and suffer anything...and which, although it is a mere mood or

85

emotion to which I can give no form in words, authenticates itself to me as the deepest determination which I possess....[12]

I cannot but be struck by the neat dovetailing of what Perry called **Commitment** and by what Erikson calls **Identity**, or in this case, **character**. The reader will note the lack of guarantee, the failure of even words to describe such a process. We have a sureness which is at one and the same time not the sureness of the dualistically infallible answer nor the lack of certitude of the relativist. Such thinking does not rule out other thought processes and conclusions; it does settle on one, however. The very settling on a commitment is seen to be part and parcel of being able to say, "This is the real me."

If one cannot arrive at committed thinking without first embracing relativistic thinking, as Perry's research indicates, the importance of academic work which insists on contextual thinking is obvious. The task of the undergraduate teacher is inevitably bound up with the student's search for identity.

C. Erikson's "Moratorium" and Perry's "Alternatives to Growth"

Eriksonian Identity theory postulates, even demands, a society-given period of delay for those undergoing a crisis of identity.[13] As Erikson sees it, most societies provide a period of permissiveness to their youth before the responsibilities of mature life begin. Such a period is characterized by a delay or pause, a time set apart. It is a time of playfulness and provocation on the part of youth; frequently it leads to a deep, if transitory commitment. It ends in a ceremonial confirmation by society, such as the presentation of a college degree.

How interesting that Perry's undergraduates often spent a period as long as a full academic year temporizing. Perry found this period to occur at various levels of development.[14] It was not necessarily seen as a time of alienation. Perry saw it rather as a time of consolidation, spreading out, a time of lateral growth. This hiatus in the process of the development of undergraduate thinking is strikingly similar to Erikson's moratorium, although it is narrower in scope. Perry reports

86

that it often takes the shape of sheer competence. The pause for breath and consolidation seems as natural for one engaged in the process of making a quantum leap in thinking processes as it does in the wider arena of seeking identity. Indeed, the two periods described by these different reporters seem to me to overlap. Erikson's telling comment that this period of youthful moratorium often ends with a deep, if temporary, commitment cannot but remind one that Perry's developmental line ends with committed thinking. Nothing in Perry's study indicates how permanent the committed thinking of his young men and women was to prove. Skeptics of Perry's work are prone to forget that impermanence and deep commitment often go together. Few undergraduates of ten years ago, for example, are presently occupied with what their area of specialty in college "prepared" them for.[15]

Note that Perry discovered three patterns of delay in his undergraduates, not just one. He sees a pattern of what he calls **retreat** in some of his subjects.[16] Although it occurs relatively rarely, it generally involves a very hostile stance toward relativistic thinking into a well-prepared niche of dualism. Perry sees it as a retreat to authoritarian submissiveness in thinking as a means for emotional peace.

It is not surprising that Perry also found that temporizing sometimes leads to what he calls **escape**.[17] The escapist thinker often begins by taking a hiatus or time of temporizing. This very time becomes encapsulated and, within the limits of the study, a permanent stage, characterized by depression, irresponsibility and relativistic thinking. It can be a period of opportunism and competency, yet it remains closed to ethical commitment. One simply doesn't want to consider values within this stance, other than the value of doing well.

These three correctives to too rosy a view of the value of a good yawn in the process of thought development serve to point up the fact that Eriksonian moratorium theory doesn't promise growth absolutely any more than Perry's alternatives do. Erikson is fully aware that some people never really emerge from their moratoria, and those who do, take the risk of emerging with a negative identity, the polar opposite of a constructive use of their talents and histories.[18] Our point is to note that both men, both students of youth, have seen a pattern of delay in the process of advancement to identity and commitment. Such a delay seems a nearly necessary prelude to further growth, but it is certainly no guarantee of it.

D. Harvard's "Party Line" and Erikson's "Monastery"

Dr. Perry makes it quite clear that the general tenor of undergraduate coursework at Harvard at the time his students were being interviewed put a strong emphasis on contextual and relativistic thinking.[19] It is quite clear that the Harvard faculty were intent on showing their students what they themselves believed to be true, namely, that all knowledge is situational, contextual, even temporary.

Erik Erikson has spoken persuasively of youth's need for ideology.[20] Erikson sees youth as a time almost demanding indoctrination in order to preserve a sense of balance and trust which once came from home. Erikson's sympathetic attitude toward the monastic indoctrination of the young Martin Luther is the most famous of his examples. Luther needed an encompassing and simple world view as a base for forming his own. The relativism of the Harvard faculty, when seen in this light, is certainly a world view, which to an undergraduate student short on both years and life experience, not to mention knowledge, cannot but be ideological. It surely smacks of indoctrination just as bluntly and just as helpfully as the indoctrination of a monk. The fact that the majority of the Harvard students learned the stance of relativistic thinking and then went beyond it to some form of committed thinking gives us a good empirical picture of a large number of young people growing toward the answer of the great question of Erikson's stage of **Identity**. That question is: "What have I got and what am I going to do with it?"[21]

E. Significance for Teachers

Our purpose is to see whether or not a study juxtaposing two such thinkers will cast light on undergraduate teaching. What can Perry/Erikson say to teachers?

1. Student as "Truth" Seeker

Erikson sees youth, whether in factory or college or elsewhere, as vitally and centrally concerned with finding "the truth."[22] Truth is seen as something worthy of trust, something worth being faithful to. It can be helpful to put this student into Perry's perspective as a person whose thinking is on the move. In a search for a message worth adhering to, the student is at the same time painfully moving from dualism to relativism and on to some form of committed thinking, with the ever-present possibility of retreating to dualistic thinking or escaping into the gamesman's position of relativist. The student may progress to learning the hard lesson of making a commitment to a person, cause, or idea with full knowledge of how situational and relativistic human learning worthy of the name inevitably is. Or, that student may take refuge in the simplicity and easiness of dualistic "right/wrong" thinking, which Erik Erikson would characterize as totalistic.[23] The path to mere competency, a life stance that ignores or refuses to deal with higher moral issues other than success is a basically relativistic stance, from a moral point of view. Success can become "the truth."

The educator who uses dualistic thinking in the classroom is promoting its use elsewhere. If one's schooling demands only memory work and simplistic thought, it is simply promoting dualistic thinking in the wider areas of life. The teacher who demands relativistic thinking in the classroom but who has no commitment to the students in front of him or her, promotes cynicism, gamesmanship, and mere competency among students.

2. The Importance of Synthetic Thinking

Erik Erikson has given us a picture of a young person embracing an ideology as something quite normal. He does not leave it at that, however. He speaks of youth as pushing a chosen message to its logical extremity, to what he calls "rock bottom."[24] It is in this process of testing that youth moves from a position of slow synthesis, a bloody and confrontive kind of synthesis. It brings world-view into the world. In Perry's language, the student would be putting his or her thought into a context and situation. If there is a difference between the two ways of looking at youth and ideology it lies in a more explicit treatment of relativism in Perry than in Erikson. Erikson's young person is not described as developmentally going through a period in which her thinking was contextual and unattached to any form of personal commitment. Although the period of Identity is seen as a time before commitment, an unattached time, my reading of Erikson does not find him focusing on relativistic thought. Erikson concerns himself more with dualisms (ideology) and commitment (identity). The shattering discovery of contextual, relativistic thinking is not treated as such in Identity development. If Erik Erikson would have us see ideological thinking as part of a developmental process, William Perry calls us to see relativistic thinking as equally important in the development of youth. For an educator to understand dualistic thinking as totally necessary in identity formation, as well as a step on which he does not encourage the student to rest, it should be equally true that the education must demand relativistic thinking, while understanding the feeling of rootlessness it generally engenders in the student. The loneliness of the student seeking commitment out of a stance of relativistic thinking is a key point in Perry's analysis.[25] It leads us to the notion of the teacher as mentor.

3. The Professor as Mentor

Erikson's classic psychohistorical study of Martin Luther gives us a penetrating look at the role of mentor, in the person of an understanding monk named Staupitz, who was Martin's religious superior when Luther was a young monk trying to find himself.[26] It was Staupitz who recognized, at just the right time, this troubled young man's genius. He not only recognized Luther's potential verbal superpower, he continually confirmed its budding existence by putting Martin to work as lecturer, exegete, and preacher. Recognition and encouragement at just the time when they were needed put this otherwise undistinguished Augustinian monk in the role of midwife to one of the towering figures of the Western World's modern era. It is interesting that Dr. Perry sees a similar need for recognition and confirmation among his Harvard undergraduates.[27] He pinpoints this need, however, localizing it in a population with its own peculiar characteristics, the young person in the relativistic world of knowledge that is ours in contemporary America.[28] Perry sees the radical nature of the process of moving from dualistic thinking to relativistic thought.[29] It is precisely the period of unattached relativism that elicits a call for mentorship from him on the part of teachers. He calls for the professor to recognize the student in that student's lonely courage as well as to confirm that lonely student in his developing thought. He sees a need for a certain community between student and teacher that is not merely the bond between authority-figure and subservient student.[30] It is a bond based on the fellowship of mutual searching engaged in by teacher and student alike. Granted the professor has more experience and expertise in her groping, yet the relationship is basically horizontal, with dignity and respect offered the student reciprocally by the professor. Within this framework, when the student asks for help from the professor, it is seen by Perry as communitarian, even egalitarian help. It provides the support of what we have chosen to call the mentor at a time of development which seriously needs such support and recognition. Erikson would point out to us that a mentor is not a friend or parent, but part of a disciplined outlook and method.[31] There is a common way of looking at things for both mentor and student, a mutuality of thinking. At the same time the mentor must have the ability to perceive, to notice, to recognize the advancing thinking processes of the student. He or she must make them, reflect them back to the student and provide work opportunities for the student in which that student will continue to grow through relativism to a hoped-for commitment unknown to either mentor or student. Just as Staupitz had no notion that he was suckling the Martin Luther, who would, with his fiery oratory, dismantle the very System which supported them both, so the professor cannot know what bent a student will eventually take—an arrangement that strikes me as as wise as it is frustrating for the professor. The notion of mentor, however, though seen by both Perry and Erikson as desirable for youth, admits of difficulties in practice.

4. Problems with Mentorship in Mass Education

It is a relatively simple matter to see that one cannot recognize or confirm those whom one does not know. The problem of vast student numbers is real. How do you act as mentor when "processing" two hundred students a year? If classes are large, how can you devise learning situations that demand or at least encourage contextual and synthetic thought? It is a commonplace in higher education that one tests large numbers by what we call "objective" tests. That's a bit of a laugher for a person whose bias as an educator is to demonstrate that there really is no such thing as objective knowledge—that all knowledge is contextual and relational. Even so, we do evaluate it by objective testing, generally demanding only dualistic thought processes from our students. The irony here would be funny, if objective testing were not so pervasive an evaluation tool in undergraduate mass education.

The mentor role has another problem. The white male teacher is still the predominant force in academe. The egalitarianism of the notion of mentorship becomes clouded when female students have, for the most part, only male teachers to choose from. To be recognized you have to have somebody who knows where you are coming from, what costs you have paid, what bridges you have crossed. Of course, perceptive mentors often cut across sexual lines as well as racial and cultural lines. But I am led to think that exceptional mentors who can transcend cultural and sexual differences are rare. Recent data on the number of male mentors having sexual relations with their female protegees leads one to think that there is often a high price to be paid for a female student seeking a male mentor.[32]

If the Sixties taught teachers anything at all about race relations, they taught us that an all-white body of teachers working with black students make condescension and racism easy. The position of mentor is so loaded with the overtones of role modelling that it seems to me to nearly demand a high percentage of mentors who can share the same sex, same cultural background, and same race with their prospective students. Let the exceptional mentors cut across these lines as they will. The need remains for ordinary folk, both mentor and student, to go the ordinary way. At present that ordinary way comes rather close to being blocked for female and minority students.

F. Summary

As I end this attempt at a useful confrontation between the two gentlemen I have chosen, it seems to call for a short summary and conclusion. I believe Erik Erikson to have been the visionary who saw the importance of dualistic thinking for youth. He saw it as a necessary launching pad for mature living and thinking. William Perry has studied the process whereby ideologies slowly become humanized and mature. That process is relativistic thinking. He has pointed out that such thinking is a necessary stepping-stone to committed thinking. Such contextual thinking carries with it a terrible burden of loneliness. Erikson has spotted for us the loneliness of the youthful ideologue and seen in his studies of great young men the invariable presence of a mentor. The same need is seen by William Perry, but within a highly focused framework, the world of the contemporary American undergraduate. His sketch of the necessary qualities of such a professor/mentor sheds light on the work of Erikson. The professor contributing to an ambience in which relativistic thought has a chance to flourish does so in the heated environment of the student's identity formation. The need for such personages is clear to me. What is not clear at all is whether there exists a pervasive enough framework in American public-supported undergraduate education for mentors to flourish and get on with the peculiar task of being whatever a mentor is. The case rests.

CHAPTER VI

KOHLBERG VERSUS PERRY ON
MORAL DEVELOPMENT

A. Introduction: Perry as Kohlberg Would Comment on Him

Ideas are like ink blots. They spread out. One idea leads to another. Another to the next. It is not difficult to explain how a study of Erik Erikson's developmental theory led to discovering William G. Perry. Perry in turn has led me to yet another developmentalist, Lawrence Kohlberg. Kohlberg's stages of moral development provide a good base from which to comment on Perry's work.

The work of both of these researchers is valuable to anyone engaged in undergraduate teaching, because both are concerned with how young people think and how their thoughts and values develop. In this chapter I want to compare these two men in the hope of pushing the reader to further comparisons, applications and syntheses. This chapter will present Perry's work with Kohlberg cast in the role of commentator.

B. Perry's Dualists and Kohlberg's Stages Three and Four

William Perry and his team undertook to examine the intellectual and ethical growth of Harvard and Radcliffe undergraduates from their entrance into college until graduation time. The study extended over a period of ten years (1954-1963). The earliest and most primitive thinking pattern that Perry found, mostly among students freshly enrolled at Harvard and Radcliffe, was a way of thinking Perry described as "basic duality." His definition follows:

The student sees the world in polar terms of we-right-good vs. other-wrong-bad. Right answers for everything exist in the Absolute, known to Authority whose role is to mediate (teach) them. Knowledge and goodness are perceived as quantitative accretions of discrete rightnesses to be collected by hard work and obedience (paradigm: a spelling test).[1]

Kohlberg's work on cognitive moral development is well known. It began with his most famous study, still in progress, a longitudinal analysis of the thinking of seventy-five American boys between ten and sixteen years of age when the study began (1956-present).[2] He has done similar studies since then in Mexico, Yucatan, Turkey, Taiwan, and other places by way of cross-cultural validation of his initial work.[3] He has studied a wide variety of populations up and down the social ladder, from prison to high school, from children to aging adults. Hence his work ranges much more widely than Perry's. His model for development has three hierarchical levels, each with two stages. I am concerning myself here primarily with Kohlberg's work on adolescents, particularly as it can be brought to bear on Perry's undergraduates. Kohlberg's second level of development in the structure of moral judgment bears many resemblances to Perry's description of dualistic thinking. Kohlberg describes this level as follows:

Maintaining the expectation of the individual's family, group or nation is perceived as valuable in its own right regardless of immediate and obvious consequences. The attitude is not only one of **conformity** to personal expectations and social order, but of loyalty to it, actively maintaining, supporting and justifying **the order** and identifying with the persons or group involved in it.[4]

In this description of "conventional" moral thinking as well as Perry's description of dualism, "Authority" is outside a person and is not subject to question. Values are fixed. There is only **one** correct way of looking at things. Both descriptions are structuralist and cognitive. Both concern themselves with **how** a person thinks rather than what.

Kohlberg has two stages for what Perry broadly labels as dualism.[5] My reading of Perry does not find this kind of distinction explicitly. Let me explain.

Kohlberg's earlier stage at this level (stage 3) is one where one's value judgments are dominated by individual people. Good behavior is that which is pleasing to others or helps them. There is conformity to what one considers "natural behavior."

His more advanced conventional stage shifts emphasis from interpersonal relationships to the wider sphere of the social order. Right behavior is seen as maintaining and conforming to society's laws.

Perry notes that his dualists are very much affected in their value judgments by their own fellow students.[6] The dormitories of Harvard were powerful sources of pressure against dualistic thinking, because the students themselves varied widely in their values and thinking processes. The persons of individual professors are likewise seen as a powerful force,[7] but the strongest pressure on dualists in the beginning comes from their peers. This is an indicator that there is some of Kohlberg's earlier stage of conventional thinking among the students, as we have described that stage above.

As I read Perry's description of dualistic attitudes gradually becoming more subtle, I note the presence of large authority groupings. Professors are referred to as a group, "they."[8] The entire university is referred to as an authority to be reckoned with.[9] Students are concerned that they seem unable to come up with contextual answers "they" ask for. Somehow, they feel that "Harvard" knows what it is doing. These are indicators of Kohlberg's more advanced level of conventionality. It fits Kohlberg's system very well that students should experience frustration if the same authority that they have grown to respect as unquestioned source of order should likewise be a force prodding them to seek academic answers that cannot be memorized, that are contextual, situational and relative.[10] Of equal note is the puzzlement of the student who discovers professors to be unabashedly at a loss to answer a query. As one student put it:

Here was this great professor, and he was groping too![11]

C. Perry's Relativists

1. Cognitive Adolescence

Perry's model makes it quite clear that the sequence of restructuring thought has as its next stepping-stone beyond various kind of dualism, a manner of thinking that he calls "relativistic." He defines relativism as follows:

> A plurality of points of view, interpretations, frame of reference, value systems and contingencies in which the **structural** properties of contexts and form allow of **various** sorts of analysis, comparison and evaluation in Multiplicity.[12]

How would Lawrence Kohlberg comment on Perry's relativism? He would call its beginning "cognitive adolescence." If relativism is a pervasive phrase through which virtually all of Perry's Harvard and Radcliffe undergraduates pass, Kohlberg would note that 50 percent of American adults never get to relativistic thinking (cognitive adolescence), and that it is extremely variable as to the time in life in which it takes place.[13]

Kohlberg sees the core of adolescence to be the discovery of the subjective self and the questioning of society's truth. I note that Perry's subjects at Harvard are described as discovering themselves and their backgrounds as part of a wide pluralism. Their experience carries with it a questioning of the society from which they come as they arrive gradually at contextual, relativistic thinking.

2. Interaction and Conflict

Kohlberg's model for movement in moral stages fits Perry's description in that the movement is based on **interaction** between the subject and his environment. Progression is not passive nor is it "wired into" biological development. It is in

98

fact a movement in conflict within the framework of community.[14]

Perry's students' whole journey from dualistic through relativistic thinking to its last phase of commitment is described in terms of interaction between student and student, between student and professor, between student and "Harvard." His description is that of a cognitive Odyssey, a journey of trials and dilemmas.

Perry's profile of the shift from dualistic thinking to relativistic thinking carries with it certain characteristics. We shall note them and see how Kohlberg's work speaks to them.

3. A Drastic Revolution

First of all, Perry sees the shift in thinking to be what he calls a "drastic revolution."[15] Kohlberg corroborates this when he places the restructuring of thought at the heart of the adolescent's discovery of his inner self and his questioning of society. This is in stark contrast to a description of adolescence tied to the development of puberty with its great emphasis on sexual reawakening. Both of our theorists center on the structural change of thought as the heart of adolescence, but Kohlberg is much more explicit in putting adolescence in the cognitive realm.[16]

4. Breakdown of Previous Guidelines and Identity

Perry sees relativism as tied to a breakdown of previous guidelines and Identity. He speaks of a terrible loneliness attendant upon the loss of absolute authority. Balancing this sense of loss is a sense of expansion in contrast with the narrowness of the past. There is a liberation attendant upon the freedom to think things out, in contrast with the former drudgery of rote memory work in studies. There is as well a new-found sense of community with relativistic peers and professors born of the realization that nobody has all the answers, all are groping—professors and students alike.[17]

Does Kohlberg comment on the breakdown of guidelines?

He does note that he believes moral relativism and nihilism are a transitional period in ethical progression between conventional morality and principled morality.[18] He quotes M.H. Podd's studies to the effect that when a person goes through an active consideration of alternative goals and value, he experiences crisis.[19]

As Kohlberg puts it:

> Essentially, then, morally transitional subjects were in transition with regard to identity issues as well as moral issues. Stated slightly differently, to have questioned conventional morality you must have questioned your identity as well....[20]

Kohlberg does not discuss the sense of expansion or its lack, of relativistic thinkers, nor does he discuss the importance of community except by implication. The implication of community needs is there, because he uses Identity explicitly in an Eriksonian sense. Erikson is on record long since on the urgency with which youth in the crisis of Identity socialize in order to discover their own Identities.[21]

5. Changed Relation to Authorities

Perry sees the relativist student at Harvard as discovering a new mutuality with heretofore revered authorities, for authority is now robbed of absolute truth. Since nobody has the final answer, all are equals by virtue of this.[22]

Kohlberg does note that adults in contemporary America used to be seen by youth as out-front conventional people, whereas today in a post-conventional society there is something new.

> What is new is the creation of a questioning providing half answers to which adolescents are exposed to their own spontaneous questioning.[23]

I think we can see the academic relativism of Harvard, as deliberately providing "half answers" to students, because from a relativistic point of view those are the only answers available to human reason. Hence the egalitarian position of professor in contrast to former absolutist days.

6. Capacity for Detachment[24]

For a dualist, intellectual detachment is a meaningless term. Authority speaks, and that is that. One doesn't break off and consider the reasonableness of it all, the importance of circumstance and other contextual factors. The relativist, on the other hand, has no authority outside. He or she is on her own, detached from her former absolutes, because she is convinced there aren't any.

Such detachment can provide a certain intellectual objectivity, hitherto unknown to the student. Because it is such a drastic change in thinking patterns, it often gives rise to a period of quiet consolidation, termed by Perry "temporizing."[25] Many of his students spent a full year absorbing the implications of their bewildering intellectual development. Some few chose to encapsulate themselves in this pattern, refusing to step beyond it. This latter, static position often took the form of relativistic competence as a final resting place. This is the position of the gamesman, an opportunistic way of thinking which excludes any form of personal responsibility for one's thoughts or deeds except for a narrowly conceived notion of success. Put in other terms, "Since all values are relative, all I have to do is my own thing."

Kohlberg is illuminating here. He finds some of his most precociously developed subjects doing an about face in moral development, going from the brink of principled behavior all the way back to a sense of justice that is preconventional.[26]

Pre-conventional morality, as the name implies, has little use for law or even inter-personal loyalty. Kohlberg likes the phrase "doing your own thing" to express one form of pre-conventional morality.[27] He mentions the case of a totally unremorseful retrogressor who had stolen a friend's watch, because he thought his friend was too trusting. Normally, neither the loyalty of friendship nor a respect for law would countenance stealing valuable property from a friend.

101

Kohlberg further notes that some of his subjects went from conventional thinking in high school back to pre-conventional in college, jumping forward again by the time they were twenty-five years old to the beginning of post-conventional thinking.

We can borrow from Perry and say that their relativism in college gave them a chance to escape responsible behavior for a while, but that this escape was indeed a transition to a further more mature outlook. "Detachment" then is viewed in a positive light by both researchers.

7. Unaware of a Path toward New Identity through Commitment.[28]

Perry's students who had become thoroughly engrossed in relativistic thinking typically went through a period when they were unaware that their relativistic thinking might ever lead to any form of commitment whatever. Religious commitment, for example, for a relativist thinker at this stage is impossible. A student seeing all religious belief as culturally relative, admitting of no absolutes, will find it does not seem rational to worship God. Nor does Perry's work show that this same subject will foresee in the midst of his or her relativism that relativistic thinking is likely to be a stepping-stone to future religious commitment.

Indeed this seems a period in which Perry's relativists were very absolute in their relativism. This kind of absolutism was found by Kohlberg's retrogressors as well. Kohlberg remarks that his extreme relativists often chose an ideology that glorified the self or an elite group. The self is seen as beyond morality, or above it.[29] The Group is "special," a law unto itself, "pre-conventional," as we have previously mentioned. I think it is safe to assume that Kohlberg's ideologues did not regard their ideologies as a step closer to maturity. They mistook ideology for maturity itself.

D. Perry's Stage of Commitment

Our picture of the college youth immersed in relativity is

complete. Perry states that nearly all of his subjects took a further step in either their third or fourth year of college. He calls this step "Commitment."

> The assumption is established that man's knowing and valuing are relative in time and circumstance, and that in such a world the individual is faced with the responsibility for choice and affirmation of life.[30]

It is tempting for the student of Kohlberg to point with delight that Kohlberg's next level of "principled thinking" is the same as Perry's "Commitment." Kohlberg speaks:

> At this level there is a clear effort to define moral values and principles which have validity and application apart from the authority of the groups or persons holding these principles and apart from the individual's own identification with these groups.[31]

1. The Age Problem

The first difficulty that strikes this read is a flat statement by Kohlberg that none of the subjects of his first famous longitudinal study has reached principled thinking at the age of twenty-three.[32] Perry does not indicate the ages of his subjects, only that they were enrolled at Harvard College in the years 1954-1963.[33] We can safely assume that the vast majority were about twenty-one years of age on graduation. Nearly all of them were "Committed' at this juncture. The data just don't match.

2. Choice versus Cognition

Furthermore, "Commitment" in Perry's thinking involves decision, choice. With Kohlberg we do not deal with decisions directly. Kohlberg measures the thinking out of which decisions come.

I do not think that "principled thinking" and "Commitment" are the same thing. Both have relativistic thought as a prerequisite, that's true. Furthermore, relativistic thinking perdures in both studies. Perry's Commitment is made in relativism. It is an act of transcendence coming from a growing sense that one must make responsible choices. It is not so much reasonable as going beyond reason. Listen again to Perry's words:

> The third solution is transcendent, taking the form of commitments. In this study the term "Commitment" refers to an act, or on-going activity in which he invests his energies, his care, and his identity...the word refers to an affirmatory experience through which the man continuously defines his identity and his involvement in the world.[34]

We are talking the language of act in a framework of relativistic thought. This central act or series of acts is basic to the adult emergence of his subjects. To refresh the reader's mind on the central significance of Identity, we quote Erik Erikson on its meaning:

> ...it occurs in that period of the life cycle when each youth must forge for himself some central perspective and direction, some working unity out of the effective remnants of his childhood and the hopes of his anticipated adulthood; he must detect some meaningful resemblance between what he has come to see in himself and what his sharpened awareness tells him others judge and expect him to be.[35]

One must ask, "If 'Commitment' is not 'principled thinking,' what is it?" In order to keep the question well defined let us take the description of how a person typically reacts after having made a Commitment in Perry's sense.

3. Reactions Immediately following Commitment[36]

Most of Perry's students reacted with an immediate sense of profound relief after their decision, the feeling of a load suddenly taken from their shoulders. They felt strongly defined as persons by their commitment. A young person having made a hard-won decision to enter medical school might say, "I am a med student." In this whole process there is a strong sense of agency, a sense of personal power in one's choice that might be expressed, "It's my choice, I did it!"

104

In my search for a comment from Kohlberg I simply do not find a personality profile for any of his stages. He discusses more how his subjects think than how they feel or act. His concern with how "they think" is based on the premise that how one thinks is the most important single factor in how one acts.[37] The sense of agency felt by Perry's subjects, however, is worthy of comment from Kohlberg's point of view.

Principled thinkers are thinkers beginning to think on matters of justice on their own. In a wide sense, all of Kohlberg's subjects are committed to justice, but the principled ones are operating on their own principles as well as those of the wider human society. His first principled stage is defined as follows:

> Right action tends to be defined in terms of general individual rights and in terms of standards which have been critically agreed upon by the whole society. There is a clear awareness of the relativism of personal values and opinions and a corresponding emphasis on procedural rules for reaching consensus. Aside from what is constitutionally and democratically agreed upon, the right is a matter of personal values and opinions. The result is an emphasis upon the legal point of view of rational considerations of social utility. Outside of the legal realm, free agreement and contract are the binding elements of obligation. This is the "official" morality of the American Government and Constitution.

Perry's subjects show a sense of agency all right, but we do not know whether or not their "Commitment" respects the rights of others; if so, to what degree? It is by no means clear that their sense of ethics is on the democratic level of the U.S. Government and Constitution.[38]

The leap to Commitment is described by Perry in terms of intuition—a Kierkegaardian leap beyond reason, or a Kantian moral imperative.[39] Reason is helpful, but it is not enough. Clearly, however, the leap is made, it is not as focussed on justice as the principled thinking of Kohlberg. It opts for a decision within the framework of reasoning but remains less defined than Kohlberg's.

105

Perry's committed juniors and seniors are young men and women who emerged from the limbo of unattached relativistic thinking to a realization that they wanted to stand for something—a set of values, a career decision, a marriage.[40] The content of the commitment remains incidental to the author's finding. He is much more interested in finding out that his subjects showed a pattern of commitment in relativistic thinking than in what they were committed to.

Kohlberg is interested in structures of thought as well as Perry, but it is peculiar to Kohlberg's findings that the structures of moral thinking his research has uncovered reveal content on the principled level, specific content universal to his subjects.

By this I mean that Kohlberg's novice principled thinkers reveal a sensitivity to the rights of other human beings that is simply not possible to contextualize away. Those rights are seen as universal.[41] A person thinks with the subtlety of a relativist, but is also capable of putting him or herself in the shoes of the rest of the populace of the world. It is this quality of enlightened empathy that is the bedrock of principled thinking.[42]

E. Summary

William G. Perry, Jr. and Lawrence Kohlberg are developmental psychologists concerned with the structure of cognitive growth as well as the structures of moral development. They both see moral development as radically dependent on cognitional structure. Perry's work is at one and the same time narrower in its focus than Kohlberg's and broader. His work is narrow because it is a ten-year study of undergraduates from the Harvard-Radcliffe complex. Kohlberg has studied moral and cognitional development in a wide variety of children, adolescents, and adults.

Kohlberg's focus is narrower, however, in that he has consistently aimed at the cognitive antecedents of moral behavior. His levels are levels of understanding. Perry's "Commitment" involves decision. Kohlberg is much more directly involved

106

than Perry in the content of moral behavior. Kohlberg's research reveals broad moral universal principles.

For the reader interested in moral development, there is opportunity for a penetrating look into the thought and value patterns of a group of elitist students in Perry's work. Kohlberg offers a more comprehensive perspective with a much wider range of articles and studies. This reader finds the two researchers shed light on each other because of their obvious parallels and differences.

If it should be that the reader finds the first brush with Kohlberg in this book to be sketchy and in need of fleshing out, well and good. The chapter that follows, a series of summations by the author on his own education, may provide the needed flesh. For one already familiar with Kohlberg, the chapter is an attempt to use his theory as a basis for commentary on the education of a Jesuit.

CHAPTER VII

REFLECTIONS ON COGNITIVE-MORAL DEVELOPMENT IN A JESUIT EDUCATION

A. Introduction: The Author and Lawrence Kohlberg

This chapter is an evaluation of my own educational experience. It includes eight years of experience in Jesuit high schools, four as a student and four as a teacher. It includes the full course of studies traditional up until recently as the course of training as a Jesuit. It carries with it experience as an undergraduate in both small and large Jesuit universities; it includes experience in five different graduate programs, all in Jesuit schools. Geographically, it is an experience that covers Midwestern and Eastern United States, North Central Europe and Central America.[1] The stance of this paper is designedly autobiographical. It is also designedly framed within the cognitive moral theories of moral development as formulated by Lawrence Kohlberg.[2] I am reflecting on an experience of education that has alternately found me as student or teacher throughout my entire adolescence and much of my adult life. It is my hope, expressed at the end of the previous chapter, that this Kohlbergian foray into autobiography will complement the more abstract treatment which precedes it.

Lawrence Kohlberg is concerned with values in education. He takes a position, in the intellectual tradition of John Dewey and Jean Piaget, that the single most important factor in moral behavior is moral judgment.[3] "You can't follow moral principles you don't have" is the gist of his stance. Another way of putting it says that how you think has a great deal to do with how you act. We are here concerned with how people think when confronted with issues of right and wrong. Kohlberg's research indicates that as a human being grows and matures, his ability to size up moral issues develops as he or she interacts with the world. Kohlberg finds that moral judgment advances in stages that follow a sequence or pattern closely following an individual's ability to reason. This sequence has been discovered to be irreversible and of a fixed order.[4] It is important for the reader to be reminded here that I am not attempting to substantiate Dr. Kohlberg's findings. Nor do I wish at the beginning of this chapter to attempt a presentation in outline of Kohlberg's whole system. My intent is to present a series of observations of my own life experience with the educational process and to let these expressions cast light on Kohlberg's theory of moral development. Let me plunge you into the world of a Midwestern Jesuit high school in the nineteen forties.

B. Reflections Stage by Stage

1. Kohlberg's Stage One

In those days many Jesuit high schools assembled their students daily in the school chapel for Mass. We all went, willy-nilly, and thought not much about it, except that it was sometimes a boring exercise. We were given to muffled laughter, continual wiggling and subdued jokes as the half hour of Mass wound down. Jesuit seminarians dutifully walked up and down the aisles of the chapel to make sure that decorum was observed. I have a vivid recollection of what sometimes happened if you got caught giggling, pinching, slouching, or passing gas. One of our prefects was nicknamed by the boys "Little Caesar." If he signalled you to get out of your pew, you knew what to expect. You quietly rose, went to the aisle and then vanished with "Caesar" out of the side doors of the chapel. Everybody inside heard a resounding crack, like a rifle shot. The unfortunate culprit would then reenter the chapel and take his place once again, his face crimson except for the white hand mark of "Little Caesar's" open palm clearly standing out on his face. This was justice. In my four years at that school there was only one "Little Caesar," but I shall never forget him. His thinking about justice was what Lawrence Kohlberg would call stage one. "The physical consequences of action determines its goodness or badness, regardless of the human meaning or value of these consequences."[5] Translated into a school situation a stage one teacher is an absolute despot. He rewards evil with brutality and feels justified in doing so. Another way of putting it is that he has little or no respect for his pupils, regarding them much as objects absolutely in his possession.

I saw a Carib school teacher once in a small primary school in Central America knock a third grade boy to the ground with a short length of knotted rope because the child was whispering to a school mate. It was a matter of justice to the teacher and he made no bones about it, although he was nervous that I might inform his higher-ups of his brutality. I mention these two incidents, because of their rarity in my own experience, but as well to show that such kinds of things are of course possible in a school. I am concerned further that the reader see these incidents as something quite different from a fit of pique or an emotional derangement. They are actions following a notion of justice, a way of thinking. The notion of "might is right" is situated on the bottom of Kohlberg's stages of moral thinking. His work indicates that all human beings begin with this most fundamental way of thinking about justice; some never get beyond it as a fundamental theoretical stance out of which they act.[6]

If I have endeavored to remember stage one moral judgments on the part of teachers in my own experience, I must remind myself that teaching is not a solitary exercise. Besides teachers there are students. Was there much stage one activity? Real brutes were rare among students even as they were rare among teachers. I don't mean to say that my high school and college classmates were never cruel to each other, but a calculated stance of physical ferocity recognizing no human convention whatever was rare. I am sure there are schools with a good number of students with this intellectual stance; we had few. I think of fraternity brutality in high school. I

111

witnessed beatings with paddles that left us black and blue on our posteriors, but put them down in large part to a desire to be "cool" on the part of the perpetrators rather than total unawareness of others as persons.

We had few savages. The atmosphere was quite different than that of Boys Industrial School in Topeka where I was a student chaplain to boys from eight to sixteen years of age. That there was an element in the school which regarded young boys as fair game for rape was clear. It was difficult to determine which boys among the rapists engaged in such activity simply because they could see nothing wrong with it. That there were some such young fellows among the many rapists practicing their arts in the toilets of the school among the little boys was clear. To argue the justice of such an act on some of the boys was a waste of time. It seemed to them that if you could get away with it, you could rape defenseless smaller boys simply because they were smaller and you were stronger. Kohlberg has found this to be true among adult prisoners in large numbers.[7] If this kind of moral judgment without regard to human convention could take as its primary form the law of talion in its most physical sense, Kohlberg categorized a more progressive notion of justice, that he still considered to be preconventional. We shall discuss this next.

2. Kohlberg's Stage Two

There is a certain back-scratching way of thinking about justice that is more reciprocal than the one we have been discussing. We are dealing with a certain quid pro quo mentality. If I scratch your back, justice demands that you scratch mine.[8] In my school, a number of seniors, a year ahead of me, spotted one of the Jesuit seminarians at a sleazy bar late on a Saturday night, a bar in close proximity to the old Grand Burlesque House. In those days, it was very unusual for any seminarian to hang around bars of any sort. To be seen in one habituated by prostitutes and drunks located in close proximity to the notorious (and doubtless quite harmless) burlesque house would have been grounds for severe discipline or dismissal for a seminarian. The delighted students who discovered the luckless seminarian struck a deal with him a few days later. In return for silence on their part, they would be given adequate grades in Latin. As far as I know, the deal was kept on both sides. It was just plain old blackmail, honorable as blackmail goes, for the ante was never upped, but blackmail it was. It was rare, but it happened from time to time. My friends who purchased passing grades in return for silence regarded it as a fair enough deal. There was not one whit of any loyalty in the arrangement, to be sure. I should not mention it as more than just a panic situation for the luckless scholastic were it not for the fact that I had occasion to know the man for a number of years as a member of the Jesuits. If he ever showed any loyalty to a student at anytime it was unobserved by me. I never mentioned to him that I knew his secret, but I think he divined it, and even in later years, as I knew him as a member of the same religious community, he was a horsetrader in his relations with the younger members of the community.

If an example of blackmail in my experience is a bit lurid, it was equally rare in occurrence. The backscratchers of a more common breed in teaching were those who demanded little of students except a certain quiet submission; in return they presented their charges with a relatively high and undeserved grade. In college we called them "an easy B." I do not mean to say that all of these men were content with this slatternly version of an academic marketplace. Some were not well; some were discouraged; but some were quite satisfied with the arrangement. It enabled them to get on with other interests with a minimum of effort in the classroom. It was a cosy arrangement, a comfortable morality devoid of professionalism, curiosity, or a sense of duty.

Among the masses of students there was a healthy amount of stage two attitudes, or at least attitudes that were tinged with it. Many of us cheated when we got the chance. Teachers who could not control us were tortured rigorously, not physically, for the most part. I have mentioned the blackmail case; the stage of morality involved there involved student as much as teacher...but there were many other cases. Every

113

year some luckless new scholastic would be driven to near collapse by students he could not control. We made noise, threw spitballs, and clowned. It was assumed that the teacher must show the students he was in charge; otherwise there was chaos. If he could charm us, put us to work, intimidate us or interest us, usually some mixture of the three, we were, for the most part, cooperative students.

3. Kohlberg's Stage Three

I have not as yet mentioned the dominant notion of justice held by the average student in my high school. It is true we had our animals and our horsetraders, but the primary and fundamental base for our morality was the notion of being "cool."[9] By and large the just man was the possessor of that elusive quality. What was cool was right; actions considered not cool, gauche, not "in" were equated with evil. It was cool to play football, and since our school was always good at football, it was cool by association to go to school there. It was cool to get good grades, provided you showed sufficient embarrassment about it. Certainly it was cool to belong to a group, whether it was being one of the guys that hung around Sherman's drug store or a member of the AO fraternity, the latter strictly forbidden by our principal. There were bands of jocks, debaters, grade hounds, the guys who worked in the library. It was cool to give teachers a hard time if you could. And of course, there were cool clothes. I want the reader to see that the morality of student chic was a progression over the preconventional ways of seeing justice in the earlier stages. Here, for the first time we have convention as an important element. You can sneer at the amusing and sometimes pathetic antics of peer pressure, but it does involve the beginnings of recognition of other people. "Cool" is a shifting phenomenon, a will of the wisp. It is as arbitrary as fashion, but it is a beginning. It is an awakening to the whole notion of convention without which human intercourse becomes very jungle-like indeed.

If my recollections both as a teacher and as a student are of

114

the dominant force in student morality as being the quality of "cool," what of the teachers?

Of course there were cool teachers with cool approaches to subject matters. By and large, teachers who attempted to be cool with the boys failed. It was hard enough for a boy to be cool; for a teacher to make a conscious effort to achieve coolness was nearly impossible. A few new teachers tried desperately to find the formula for making themselves liked by being hip or cool, but for the most part they failed so miserably that they became endowed immediately with damning nicknames indicative of their efforts. How well I remember Sexy Jim. Obviously this young seminarian thought it was cool to talk sex with boys. True, the boys talked of sex in cool terms among themselves, but you had to know just how to do it. Sexy Jim failed miserably and was branded for his entire stay at our school with that derisive name. Overt efforts to be liked were greeted by the boys with equal derision. For a teacher to be friendly to a boy in any way but the gruffest was to invite the boy to be accused of being a "brown nose" by his peers. I won't go into the origins of the term "brown nose," but its more polite equivalent of apple-polisher was totally uncool from the point of view of the boys.

It is true that we had teachers we thought were cool. There was a priest who could punt a football fifty yards with his cassock on. I remember the day he strolled into the school basement where a group of us were training for the school boxing tournament. Tucking up the corners of his soutane into his cincture he casually asked for a skip rope. Wow! He could skip forward, backwards, two at a time, cross his hands while skipping, exactly like the fighters we had seen in movies. The whole demonstration took about two minutes. He handed me the rope with a grin and walked out. He never came back, never mentioned it in class and never told us of his boxing career. He got a kick out of doing it, I'm sure, but doing that momentously cool thing was not important to him and we knew it. It wasn't important to Father Tom Kelly to be cool and we knew it. THAT was cool.

4. Kohlberg's Stage Four

If being cool was the summation of the law and the prophets for most of the kids at THE high school, and that's what we called it, it was **not** the dominant morality of the faculty. With "them" it was the law.[10] There was a priest we kids called "Kissy" Coles because he had heavy lips like a character in a comic strip...and, of course, because he was not kissy at all.

Father Coles taught English. When he taught me, he had a small book of rules of English grammar, composed by himself and mimeographed. I don't think there were forty pages in that book, in marked contrast to the incredibly prolix and weighty publishers' editions of grammars that were standard fare for most of my high school English classes. Kissy made it clear to us that we would be required to learn that book by heart and to apply the simple rules of grammar contained in it. We covered the whole book in the first two months of school as he told us we would. He tested us every week on the contents of that book from the first week of school until the last day of school in June. His assignments were short, but regular. Father Coles was not an abusive man. The closest to striking a boy I ever saw him come was a whack on the top of the head with a rolled-up magazine. He made no deals with us. He certainly did not care one whit whether he was cool or not. Above all, he didn't care whether we were cool or not. He cared that we learn his grammar rules and that we could apply them in writing prose. Any mistake in spelling we made in a composition had to be done over five times on our homework for the rest of the year. He would not tolerate any form of paper or heading that was not the standard one he explained to us on the first day of class. Handwriting that was even remotely unclear was returned with the simple command that it be redone for the next class. "Colesie's" little black book, which he carried on his person at all times, had every bit of extra work each of his students had to do carefully inscribed in it. I, for one, realized in the first two weeks of school that I would save myself endless trouble by sitting down and memorizing what he wanted as well as doing his moderated written assignments with the utmost care. Others in my class were slower to see that Coles was deadly in earnest and that there was no way out of learning the law except at cost of an escalating series of corrective assignments for recalitrant types who figured it was cool to be sloppy or late or inexact.

I had occasion, years later, to teach in the same high school with Father Coles in a different city. He was just as I had remembered. Many of us on the faculty relied on him to shape up the first year students, and shape them up he did. Nor was he content with confining his activities to the classroom. "Colesey" was a great walker. On free afternoons he would walk to the homes of boys who were resisting his efforts and appear like a clap of thunder at their homes. There he was as intransigent with the parents as he was with the boys. His blunt and unexpected appearances on doorsteps and on the telephone left many a parent as dumbfounded and sometimes enraged as he left his students. The football and basketball coaches found him anathema. He kept those who did not know or apply the laws of English grammar after school regardless of their importance in athletics. When it came to a showdown between the coaches and "Colesey," arbitrated by the principal, Coles generally came off first. This grim and generally unsmiling man was a symbol of something very important in the school where I was a student and in another one where I taught with him as a colleague. I do remember him grinning as he swirled down a long terrazo school corridor, gaunt in his black soutane, black notebook in hand. Warhorse that he was, he quoted to me the famous taunt of the French at Verdun thrown at the advancing German army, "They shall not pass!"

If Father Coles typified an approach to teaching that paid great attention to the written law, what effect, you may ask, did this have on the students?

Most of us had the attitude of Miniver Cheevy toward the Medici—

> Miniver loved the Medici,
> although he had never seen one
> He would have sinned incessantly

117

could he have been one.
E.A. Robinson, *Miniver Cheevy*

We would have all "sinned incessantly" to be cool. But Father Coles introduced us to something beyond being cool. He introduced us to a correct and orderly way of doing things whether cool or not. I have used Coles as a symbol, for the three Jesuit schools I have taught in and the many others I have had contact with were permeated with a sense of law. The best of them insisted successfully on lawful and exact English, Mathematics, Latin, Modern Languages, and until recently, Religion. We learned the law as a challenge to being cool. It was a more reasoned convention.

It is important to recognize that a progression of moral judgment in Kohlberg's scheme of things is sequential. Students at Kohlberg's stage one or two would find a law-and-order understanding of morality nonsensical.[11] The inviolability of the written law makes no sense to someone who has yet to understand any kind of convention whatever. Those who have begun to understand convention, no matter how ephemeral the convention of "cool" may be, are in a position to begin to understand a more stable convention.

Did the students I knew both as a fellow and as a teacher actually rise above the ethic of cool during their high school years? I believe a good number of them did.

I recall when I was a teaching seminarian that our principal called a meeting of the entire student body, five hundred strong, in the school auditorium. There had been some vandalism at a football game, unusually raucous screaming from the stands, rumors of an impending rumble between the Rockhurst boys and our hated rivals, the boys from the Christian Brothers School, De La Salle. To my own amazement, Dick Corrigan, a senior and starting tackle on the football team, approached our principal as he was about to enter the auditorium and asked for permission to address the assembled students. Dick asked that every single member of the faculty, including the principal, leave the hall. Leave we did. Fifteen minutes later the doors opened and a more subdued group of young men I have never seen quietly left the hall and quietly went to their classrooms. Exactly what happened I shall never know; the boys were rather close-mouthed about it all. One of them, not normally noted for his seriousness, told me rather tersely that Corrigan gave them a reading out the likes of which the principal would never have dreamed of. Dick Corrigan, one of the coolest young men in the school, had become a man of the law.

If Corrigan's conversion was dramatic, there was evidence of less sensational change among many of the older boys. I had a crew of "elders" who took attendance in a huge and potentially unruly study hall and who monitored the behavior of the smaller boys when I permitted them to leave the study hall to use the school library. Freshmen who tried cribbing homework from one another in the library often found themselves escorted to my desk by a grinning senior. In the locker rooms at the gymnasium I learned soon enough that older grant-in-aid students were a far more effective preventative measure against stealing than I was. They enforced the law, and although the younger boys did not like it, my co-policemen were not looked down on. Mind you, I only chose helpers who were already well established as cool. By and large the boys who loved the school and who were leaders among the student body had come to understand that the law of the Jesuit school was a good one. Most of them did not question it, but they saw it as a better way of ordering their school lives than the shifting sands of the morality of being cool.

5. Kohlberg's Stage Five

You may suspect that obedience to the law is not seen by Lawrence Kohlberg as the pinnacle of moral maturity. It may be understood as the peak of what he calls conventional morality, but his work had led him further.[12] In his hierarchy of forms of moral judgment, he sees the next step as a more reflective one. In stage five right and wrong are perceived in terms of democratic procedure with many possible answers to a given moral dilemma. The duly arrived at consensus of the people is what constitutes the law. One cannot arrive at such an understanding without the mental ability to see a number

119

of answers to a single question. One must have the capacity to see a given problem from a number of different sides. The law-and-order mentality is more simplistic. It tends to intellectualize in black and white terms. In questions of morality, there is a right answer and a wrong one. The law has the right answer, and that's that. My first brush with a body of teachers who took the democratic model to moral issues occurred when I was thirty-four years of age. I had been sent to study religious and pastoral education at a small international Institute in Brussels, Belgium called "Lumen Vitae." Most of my religious training up to that point had laid heavy emphasis on the law; the law was the deciding factor in settling moral issues. In Brussels we discovered a new authority. Our new understanding of the Church we studied was heavily democratic.[13] We studied the Church as "The People of God." We looked at theological teachings as having little meaning unless they coincided with the "sense of the faithful." Active participation in Church worship was founded on the "priesthood of all the people." My somewhat eroded but still active sense of the inviolability of the law in itself was hammered unmercifully by scholars of my own Church three hours every morning, six days a week. It was a giddy vision, a terrifying one in its calls for responsibility, traumatic and joyful all at the same time. For me at least, much of its power lay in its reasonableness. The democratic Church, to sum it up, was presented by a variety of scripture scholars, psychologists, historians, and theologians whose erudition as a group surpassed any group of teachers I have had before or since. They encouraged us to think about our thinking. Bernard Haring told us flatly that the Pope could not speak out against birth control with any degree of authenticity, because the understanding and practice of the people had already accepted it. Liturgical scholars told us that the priest **presided** over the Mass, that public worship was something that was basically communal. Francis Durwell painstakingly explained to us that a Christianity that made a distinction between soul and body in effect denied the Resurrection of Jesus. We asked

120

ourselves, "If our bodies are so holy why did all of us priests, sisters, and brothers take vows of perpetual virginity?"

It was a heady year. In Kohlberg's terms, it was a stage five year. Had we had no understanding or respect for the law, it could not have occurred. At its best, the change wrought by that year was one that occurred because the cognitional ground for it had been well prepared. Most of the students in that small institute were mature people ranging in age between twenty-five and forty. We had been chosen by religious authorities from countries all over the world as people who had held posts of responsibility and were loyal to our churches. We were middle-of-the-roaders, company persons, people of the law. Kohlberg would have said that we were ripe for a new understanding.

If I have described firsthand, however briefly, a transition from a conventional morality to the beginnings of a post-conventional one, I hope that the reader has not missed the pain and loneliness of my brief description. I remember well the realization that I had no longer a ready-made authority on which to make my decisions. The best I could do was to use my own head and to talk interminably with my friends. There were no more teachers with a capital T. The many discussions we had with our professors were quite egalitarian. These learned men and women were probably more scholarly than any teachers we had ever had, but their very persuasiveness turned them into more learned equals and fellow searchers ...fellow members as we put it, of "The People of God." That we should have seen a **variety** of answers to basic questions, having seen only a **few** before, was a shock. Imagine if you will a similar shock, should it have occurred, when we were high school students or college undergraduates!

We left our discussion of the Jesuit high school as inhabited largely by two rather winning groups of boys, the cool ones and those who had recently discovered the law. What of those who saw further? The cognitional research of Piaget and Kohlberg, among others, assures us that young persons in their late teens are often capable of seeing multiple answers to basic questions.[14] Intellectually, they are often capable of going beyond a simple acceptance of the law. In the jargon of the trade, they are capable of relativistic thinking. Where were the relativists, you may ask, in those high schools where I studied and taught? Of course, they were there. They were unacknowledged often; and they usually didn't fit in, but they were there.

If you were a young man who saw that there might be other ways of doing things than the Jesuit way, then what? What if you hated football AND debate? What if you wondered whether being a Catholic was such a big deal? What if you questioned the standard sexual morality? What if you thought music or art were of greater interest and had more to say than grammar, math and literature? In fine, what if you were a young philosopher, trying to put your own order into your world? In my schools in the Forties and Fifties, you were smack up against the law. Except for an occasional very understanding prof, there was no one who understood you and there was no place for you.

Every school has its interstices, mind you, its places of asylum for young philosophers. Those interstices were generally not cool places and they were often illegal. Where I taught there was a forbidden fraternity in which one could find a few philosophers. The football managers were not cool, but they were acceptable and original boys for the most part. There were philosophers too, who became adept at the art of camouflage. On the outside they were absolutely straight in whatever the cool clothing happened to be. They observed the externals of the school rules. On the inside and away from the enforcers of the law, they were rather remarkably nonconformist. The lesser and more lonely sports had their freaks too: boxers, rifle team members, even track men. There was a basic problem of finding associates who were acceptable both to the school rules and to the student law of cool.

There was, in addition to the problem of the student philosopher finding a suitable crack in the framework, an even larger problem. Kohlberg has noted that when the beginnings of relativistic thinking occur at the same time in life as the crisis of identity, there is often a rather dramatic if short-lived regression in moral thinking.[15] I made a point of noting that the relativists of the Churchy circles of the Lumen Vitae Institute were, most of them, mature people who had found a niche in life, an identity if you will, from which vantage point they could deal with the turbulence of change within the Roman Catholic Church.

That vantage of an achieved identity is virtually impossible for a high school boy. He just hasn't grown that much yet. To put it briefly, the philosophers were often the animals. Call it what you want, the mixture of intellectual development and identity crisis often caused a good old regression in terms of moral maturity. The film **Animal House** with its destructions, con jobs, and other social outrages placed in the early Sixties struck me as a beautiful example of what I'm talking about. The kids wrecking cars, flunking out of school, fighting, eating and chasing girls were often the thoughtful ones. Our theoretician would call them stage two people, back-scratchers. They were common types in my schools in the Forties and Fifties. They were not welcome then in Jesuit schools and I don't think they are welcome now.

If there is tragedy involved in the school's treatment of such difficult folk, it is the failure of most institutions to recognize them for being very perceptive and often very troubled. The lack of institutional machinery to put the student philosophers to work as questioners discovering that there is a plurality of answers to many questions is still with us. Kohlberg dares to say that in order to challenge these young people there must be within the school a real form of democracy.[16] A law-and-order institution did not help them, and if Kohlberg is right, it never will. I want to leave solutions until later in this paper, so we will leave the budding student philosopher as either a young and frustrated democrat, or in his more traumatized version, a perceptive but temporary back-scratcher and blackmailer. There is another moral state in Kohlberg's scheme of things, beyond the principled people who rely on the consensus of their fellow human beings.

6. Kohlberg's Stage Six

In Kohlberg's sixth and final moral stage what is right is defined by a decision of conscience in accord with certain far-reaching and universal principles.[17] A perfect example of such a broad principle may be found in the Scriptural injunction "You shall love the Lord your God with all your heart, and with all your soul, and with all your strength, and with all your mind; and your neighbor as yourself."[18]

Such a principle of universal concern for human life does not depend on democratic procedures; it is not altered or subject to alteration by ballot, or due process of law. It is not subject to revision should it not be cool. It is not changed by a promise of favors or the threat of physical punishment. Persons operating from a stage six vantage in their morality are meditative, thorough folk, given to abstract thinking, fully aware of the relativism of most moral injunctions. I can still recall one of my favorite teachers telling me, "Francis, the only form of moral evil not condoned somewhere in the Bible is killing for your own pleasure!" That was a retort to a comment about the inerrancy of the Bible in regard to moral teaching. The principled moral person knows the ambiguity and contradictions of any body of moral directions and yet holds to certain bed-rock principles applying them rigorously to situations as they come up.

To spot such an attitude of mind in a teacher is not always easy. Oftentimes such teachers seem arbitrary. One of my old mentors once said of himself "that he had not been given the grace to bear fools patiently." He was irritated by and irritating to folks who wanted simple answers. He delighted in cornering them, in showing them the contradictions of their answers...he refused as well to provide any answers of his own. A regular feature of his philosophy class was to spend an entire class proving beyond a shadow of a doubt that a philosophical position held water. The next day he would stride into class, his eyes gleaming, and show that everything he said the day before was false. The protests of the anguished note-takers in front of him were answered by his chortling delightedly, "Just because I said that yesterday doesn't mean I'm going to say that today." He wasn't very helpful when it came to reviewing for exams. We had dutifully learned that we had free will and that we did not, that some people had it and that some did not, that nobody was free all the time, that some people were free some of the time, that some ages in life were freer than others, that nobody knew really what freedom was anyway, that even a child could see and understand the meaning of freedom. Memorizing your way into one of Father William Wade's tests just couldn't be done. Toward the end of the semester or before a big exam he used to tell us that he could teach the whole course in fifteen minutes. He would furiously and contemptuously write a beautiful summation of one standard Thomist position on human freedom on the blackboard in perfect order as an offering for those who refused to think, and stride from the room laughing at the stupidity of his own logic. Many of his students wondered if he himself stood for anything at all, but there were signs.

He genuinely tried to avoid embarrassing us in public. I remember learning to my amazement that the students he used to "pick on" in class were carefully selected contentious souls. He argued with students who could take it and was very gentle with the unsure ones, the easily affronted, and the timid. Nobody escaped his carefully planned confusion, but the up-front arguments in class were reserved for a very few. If he really blew up in class, which was quite a show in itself, he invariably apologized the next day. Slowly some of us realized that he really did want us to think; if he couldn't make us think, he could at least corner us in our obvious stupidities. If he did not advertise what his principles were, it was partially because he **was** a good teacher. I know he figured that if he had to tell us what he stood for, it would be just one more exercise of note-taking on our part. If we wouldn't figure out how a priest could stand up in a classroom of seminarians and prove to us that there was no God, that was our problem. I have chosen this man as a stage six teacher, because he was one of the very few teachers I have ever had in my life who challenged me to think. He knew, as well as Lawrence Kohlberg, that "thinking about your thinking" is a necessary condition for any kind of moral maturity, but he wouldn't tell us so. We had to discover **that** ourselves. I am morally certain that a good half of the students he ever taught thought he was really a cool teacher, so explosive, so dynamic, such a character—but that it really was impossible to take notes from the man. "He just wasn't very organized." Were he living today and I were to tell him that I was writing him up as a principled man, I have no doubt he would prove me wrong and thoroughly enjoy doing so.

If principled teachers are rare in my experience, it will come as no surprise to the reader that students who have arrived at a morality built around universal ethical principles are much rarer still. I am tempted to say that for a student to operate at a stage six morality is a contradiction in terms. The classrooms I have sat in would have made persons in Kohlberg's final stage uncomfortable...and yet I have studied with older students both as an undergraduate and a graduate student. I am prepared to say that I have never been in a college or university situation where the majority of the students functioned at stage six.

My own experience of fifteen years of Jesuit formal training and several more years of schooling as a Jesuit after the regular course of studies has convinced me that the men of my time were very slow to arrive at principled thinking of the most autonomous kind. Our training was very long; much of it was very insular, apart from confrontation with people who differed from us. There were a few men who entered the Jesuits in their late twenties or early thirties; almost all of them left after a short time. Those who stayed struck me as men of great patience. Those who slowly, over a period of nearly two decades, arrived at what Kohlberg would call stage six thinking were truly remarkable men.

We knew about them, but in the regular course of studies they were normally shunted away from the seminarians. The

Society of Jesus is a stage four organization that has to its great credit a long-standing intellectual tradition that has always allowed for its share of characters, including intellectual characters. It is most understandable that the best minds of the Jesuits have normally been carefully kept away from the young men in training. To put it in Kohlberg's frame of thought, the Jesuits operating on the highest level of morality are kept away from the younger men. When we were seminarians we knew of the "independents"; if they wrote books, we read the books; often we aspired to be like them. I remember once wangling a summer working for Father Harold Rahm in a youth center in El Paso. Rahm was one of the independents; it was no accident that El Paso was about as far away from any Jesuit house of studies in his own Province as geography would permit. The day I got off the train he drove me around the desperately poor area of El Paso where he worked with children and teenagers. He gave me a little pep talk on saying my prayers while I was there for the summer while assuring me that he was proud to be a Jesuit as well as expecting a lot from me because I was one too, though still in my training. "S.J. is good enough for me," he said. He told me to keep the Jesuit rule while I was there too, and it surprised me to be told that from the likes of Harold Rahm. I knew he was no seminary type.

And I remember gasping when he said rather casually, "I keep the rule myself; I do what they tell me, except when the rules come between me and my people. Then I fight 'em." That was a new line for me. I don't think I had ever before heard any of "my people" put morality ahead of the Jesuit Rule as a matter of factly as that. I was the last Jesuit scholastic that ever worked for Harold Rahm. You just couldn't go saying things like that among the younger men, let alone living those things. Rahm did both. The point of this seeming digression is that as the Jesuits of my time slowly matured, some of them became really autonomous men. Those who did seldom were allowed much contact with the younger men in training. Our official morality did not allow for it. Stage six people by definition function above the law and therefore are dangerous to it. In my own Jesuit organization they were tolerated often, generally persecuted to some degree, and usually honored after they were dead. I say in defense of the Jesuits that no organizations function at stage six, and few at stage five. Truly moral people inevitably suffer at the hands of government in any organization; they never quite fit. In the parlance of education, stage six people are always colleagues with their teachers, even if they are cast in the role of student. Stage six students are just teachers who happen to be on the other side of the desk. They are not impressed by anything except reason, and of course, they tend to be embarrassing in a classroom. They know too much!

C. Conclusions: Utilities and Warnings

I have run the gamut of stages of teachers and students in my own life experience. The conclusion of this essay will be an attempt to state briefly what I have learned from my experiences as formalized in the Kohlberg model. Here are my conclusions.

Stage one teachers are resented by all students. They are basically destructive people. For students living the morality of being cool, this kind of teacher is especially lethal. This teacher is totally unaware that public embarrassment of a student living at stage three is the near equivalent of capital punishment.

Stage two teachers can be equally destructive to the "cool" student, but at least they require provocation of some kind. Their total lack of loyalty to students, however, cripples them as teachers of youth. Kids need to be loved.

Stage three teachers are terribly vulnerable to the student acting at levels one and two. They are usually pathetically unsuccessful in being cool to the cool culture. Those who do succeed are educational and moral faddists. They are here today; tomorrow they are forgotten or laughed at.

Stage four teachers can be effective in working with kids at level three. They tend to be overly rigid, however. Fanatics have a hard time in a school, because they arouse such resentment among students and colleagues. Stage four morality has the aura of fanaticism around it.

Stage five teachers can be effective in helping the "cool" ones learn the progression to a more ordered conventionality. Those teachers understand the need of law, but they are not slaves to it and hence are capable of tolerance. They can appreciate both different kinds of students and different kinds of teachers. They tend to be good principals in secondary schools.

Stage six teachers are very rare. They tend to be misunderstood by both school systems and students. Those who have the patience to deal with preconventional students and conventional students are truly remarkable people. They are capable of opening whole new vistas of thinking to a great variety of students. They are sometimes the best of teachers. However, their own sense of frustration with the obtuseness of others often undercuts their effectiveness with students operating below stage five. Normally they are not found in administrative educational posts. When they are there, they are either superb or disastrous. The true innovators in the world of education, like most principled innovators, are generally crucified, have a few perceptive followers, and have more influence after they are laid in the tomb than before.

The very last word in this essay is a kind of farewell reminder to the reader. These reflections are personal. They are limited to one man's experience. The people in all of them are real. Granted, they have been re-membered in this essay, perhaps dismembered. The only conscious alterations with my perceived reality have been slight changes in the names of some of the people I discuss.

I have placed my generalizations in summary form at the end of my remarks better to enable the reader to separate the wheat from the chaff. I shall further confess that I have not asked for Lawrence Kohlberg's imprimatur for these thoughts. It is up to the reader to go about separating wheat and chaff as well as giving imprimaturs. My purpose will be satisfied if I have deepened the reader's understanding of Kohlberg, begun in more abstract form in the chapter before this one. This bit of a teacher's autobiography may serve as well as a bridge to the next chapter. There we treat formally just how one might teach cognitive-moral development in college.

CHAPTER VIII

TEACHING COGNITIVE-MORAL DEVELOPMENT IN COLLEGE

Most of the previous chapters in this book have concerned themselves with promises. A university, despite the odds, is seen as a promising place for education. Small groups hold much promise for learning in the undergraduate classroom. Even the ethics of the teacher in the classroom are seen to promise the birthing of student knowledge. Erik Erikson and William G. Perry, Jr. promise us earnestly that we can expect much from an undergraduate if we understand his or her path of intellectual development. Lawrence Kohlberg's stages hold forth the prospect of an ever more precise understanding of the student's moral development. The author's own education, studies from Kohlberg's point of view, challenges the professor to improve on the model presented. Promises! Promises!

At this point the author feels an actual course presentation is called for. Chapter Four's journal has given an unvarnished look into a teacher's classroom. This chapter aims at describing a whole course in as great detail as possible. It is the author's vision of the reality that lies beyond the promises of theoreticians.

The chapter is concerned with presenting a way for teaching moral development to undergraduate college students. Its prime base is the work of Lawrence Kohlberg.[1] William G. Perry's study of intellectual and ethical development among undergraduates will be used to lay the ground for understanding Kohlberg.[2] Erik Erikson's work will be used to study moral development during the crisis of Identity.[3] Elisabeth Kubler-Ross will be used to deepen the insights gained from Kohlberg, Perry and Erikson.[4]

My approach seeks to be faithful to Kohlberg's theory, but it seeks as well to take the stance of the generalist. I do not hesitate to make use of other disciplines than developmental psychology. In fact, strong emphasis is laid on the use of literature as a vehicle for posing moral dilemmas as well as shedding light on moral development. I choose to incorporate the religious and philosophical elements that come into play in the literature I use. I will open with a brief description of Kohlberg's position on moral development.

A. Components and Antecedents of Moral Development

1. Cognitive Components and Antecedents

The cognitive-developmental approach to moral development as seen by Kohlberg has a number of componential underpinnings.[5] The most salient of these is the parallelism between logical and ethical development. The development of moral judgment depends upon intellectual development. Kohlberg does not attempt to develop a model for intellectual development himself but is quite content with the work of the epistemologist Jean Piaget.[6] He is concerned that one sees that moral development and intellectual development, although parallel, are not the same thing. He puts it succinctly: "...you can be smart and never reason morally."[7]

Intellectual development is not "wired into" moral judgment. Moral judgment must be accompanied by social interaction with, and stimulation by, persons at a more advanced level of moral maturity. Kohlberg insists on the word "interaction." Mere presence is not enough. There must be active intellectual exchange with more advanced people before one can progress in moral judgment development.

2. Affective-Volitional Components and Antecedents of Moral Judgment Development

Although convinced that moral maturity contains certain

universal principles cutting across cultural lines,[8] Kohlberg by no means feels that ethical development is some sort of blind automatic emotional maturation. His research shows how one **reasons** about right and wrong to be paramount in moral judgment. I can, for example **feel** anxious about stealing for a great many different **reasons**.[9] Feelings and desire are secondary in his model for moral development.

3. Social Role-Taking Components and Antecedents of Moral Judgment Development

Kohlberg feels that the ability to walk in another persons' shoes, so to speak, is basic to developing moral judgment. As he puts it:

> The primary meaning of the word "social" is the distinctively human structuring of action and thought by **role-taking**, by the tendency to react to others as like the self, and to react to the self's behavior from the **other's point of view**.[10]

Moral development depends on one's opportunity to react to one's own behavior from the other's point of view. Our author sees an environment which provides such opportunities as one in which the individual has a sense of participation and membership in the group to which he or she belongs. To develop, one needs to be able to take an **active part**. One needs a meaningful voice in group decision-making. In short, the group most conducive to understanding the role of others is basically democratic.

4. Justice Components and Antecedents of Moral Judgment Development

Even in the most primitive stage of moral development, where justice is understood as "an eye for an eye and a tooth for a tooth," there is role-taking. Kohlberg's four-year-old son is described by his father as at this stage.[11] The little boy was a vegetarian, because he didn't want to kill animals. When his father told him a story about Eskimos killing seals for food, the little boy showed his colors. He decided the Eskimos were evil because they killed seals. Because of their injustice toward

133

seals, he decided he would make one exception on his diet of vegetables. He would henceforth eat Eskimo meat, given the opportunity, thus evening the score with the "bad guy" Eskimos. The point of the story is, of course, that one can at one and the same time feel empathy and have a sense of justice that is primitive.

There is a further point. Lawrence Kohlberg's child was a member of an institution, the institution of the Kohlberg family. The level of justice understood and practiced in the institution has, according to our author, a great deal to do with the moral development of the members of the institution. These are his words: "The formation of a sense of justice requires participation in just institutions."[12]

It was precisely the family of the child that showed him the conflict of roles between Eskimo and seal. The little boy's participation in this institution allowed him to make his own judgment, now a more sophisticated one than before, even if it did solve the problem by deciding that eating Eskimos was just. Had the problem of the Eskimo hunter never been posed, the child's vegetarianism would have remained an empathic position but safe from the complicating factor of the Eskimo hunter. Kohlberg's encouraging the little boy to think about an answer to the problem is an indicator of the high level of institutional justice in the family, allowing the boy the chance to transform and reflect upon his vegetarianism.

We have now reviewed the basic components and antecedents of moral development—congnitional factors, affective ones, role-taking, and institutional factors. Before plunging into the college classroom we need to review the stages of development themselves.

B. Kohlberg's Moral Stages in Brief[13]

1. Punishment and Obedience. What gives me physical pleasure is right. Anything that is wrong is defined in terms of physical punishment. Motto: "Might is right."

2. Instrumental Relativist. Rightness is understood in terms of a fair price. Revenge is just if it is measured in terms of the offense. Motto: "Tit for tat."

3. Interpersonal Concordance. Good behavior is what pleases significant others. Being "bad" is what causes displeasure to those for whom I feel loyalty. Motto: "My friends are everything."

4. Law and Order. Good behavior is understood as keeping the law. Evil is breaking the law. Motto: "America, love it or leave it."

5. Social-contract legalism. Right action is understood in terms of other individuals' rights and the consensus of society. Motto: "By the people, for the people, of the people."

6. Universal Ethical Principle. Right action depends upon rational argument and self-chosen ethical principles. Evil is seen in terms of my own conscience. Motto: "I stand alone."

The outline above is meant to be a reminder to the reader, rather than an attempt at doing what Kohlberg has already done. More complete descriptions of Kohlberg's work occur in earlier chapters of this book. A further reminder is in order. The meaning of the term Kohlberg uses for all his six divisions of development is of paramount importance. He refers to his six "moral stages."[14] These stages are found to occur always in the same sequence. The first must always go before the second. The second before the third, etc. Each stage is seen as **qualitatively** different from each other stage. Kohlberg refers to each separate stage as a "structural whole."[15] One's ability to understand another's point of view differs qualitatively from stage to stage.

Furthermore, stages are seen to be "hierarchical integrations." What is implied here is that higher stages **include** lower ones. A person can understand the stages he or she has advanced through. Subjects prefer higher stages right up to the stage they are in as more adequate morally. Not surprisingly, they have some understanding or desire to reach more than one stage beyond their present one.

C. Kohlberg in the Classroom

So much for a refresher or reminder of the cognitive-developmental theory of morality according to Lawrence Kohlberg. The next stage in this chapter is to take the theory and describe how to put it to work on an undergraduate classroom.

1. Kohlberg's Own Undergraduate Teaching

Our professor has described briefly his own excursions into moral development among university undergraduates,[16] but the brunt of his own work in formal schooling remains on the secondary level.

He does indicate that he and his associates at Harvard offered a General Education course called "Political and Ethical Choice."[17] In part the course consisted of a series of small group discussions of moral dilemmas, from "Should I steal medicine to save my dying wife?" to situations more au courant, "Should I be faithful to my sexual partner?" The method of approach was Socratic:

> ...the use of questions, as employed by Socrates, to develop a latent idea, as in the mind of a pupil, or to elicit admissions...[18]

Small group discussions showed students to be challenged and stimulated by other students making moral judgments at a level a stage above their own. A student whose judgment as to the morality of sexual fidelity was dominated by the theory of pleasing his or her partner (stage 3), often found him or herself challenged by a student who responded to sexual fidelity in terms of ideology or law (stage 4). On the other hand, stage four students were seldom challenged or intrigued by responses of a level **below** their own. The experience of challenge was thought-provoking and over a semester's period stimulated many students to revise and reintegrate their moral judgments one stage upward. It is intriguing to note that in these discussions there is evidence that in some cases an active directing role on the part of the teacher was not ncesssary:

> In the **leaderless** groups with higher interest in discussion, upward change was about as great as it was in the teacher-led groups.[19]

Briefly then, I note Kohlberg's classroom experiments in both high school and college center around conflicting solutions to moral questions in the framework of discussion. His teaching model is a very active one, the Socratic questioner probing, the defender continually being challenged.

2. My Adaptation of Kohlberg to the Classroom

My aim is to demonstrate **one** man's Socratic method to the reader of this paper. I want to show how I do it, for there must be many tactics within the grand strategy of involving the student in moral dilemmas. Back we go then, to Kohlberg's components and antecedents to moral judgment development.

D. Step by Step—Teaching Kohlberg's Components

1. Engaging the Student in Cognitive Development

If the essence of Kohlberg's understanding of moral development is intellectual, it is with intellectual growth that I feel I must start. My first aim is to get my students to think about the way they think.

We begin with the showing of a film entitled "Hunger in America,"[20] a survey of different groups of people in the United States who are badly undernourished. We see a graphic picture of a government official who says flatly that poor people are poor (hence undernourished) because they are lazy. We hear a farmer, whose children stare blankly at the photographer, explain that he's proud to be poor. God made him poor, and that's good enough for him. We view case after case of people oversimplifying the problem of malnutrition. Both those who are hungry and those charged with helping them make sweepingly simplistic statements. I stop the film frequently and ask the students to examine the logic of, for example, the farmer who said, "God made me poor, and I'm proud of it." It does not take long for the class to see dualistic thinking among the people in the film, and in this case how it is fostered by their churches. It is easy to show in class that most problems have more than one right answer and one wrong answer. It is much more difficult to have the student see his own dualistic thought. Put another way, it is easier to think about someone else's thinking than it is to think about your own.

137

In keeping with a rhythm alternating concrete case presentation with presentation of theory, I explain formally the results of William G. Perry, Jr.'s ten years of work examining the thinking of Harvard and Radcliffe undergraduates.[21] A two-page summary of Perry's three developmental stages of thinking is the reading material. We have already studied dualistic thinking in the film. Perry's work shows that the simple, black-and-white thinking he calls dualism generally gave way to a more contextual kind of thinking among his undergraduate subjects. They went from a kind of reasoning which saw only one legitimate "right" answer to the realization that serious questions in any academic discipline do not admit single, absolute answers. This new mode of thinking Perry refers to as "relativistic." At heart, it is seen as a manner of thinking which sees many legitimate answers to questions of almost any sort. It demands that the thinker put both question and answer in contexts of varying kinds.

Perry's third stage of development, "committed thinking," can only occur when an individual has seen the complexity of knowledge. A grasp of human knowledge as relative and contextual must occur before one can think in a committed way. Committed thinking involves choosing a good answer among many good answers. It does not exclude all answers but one as correct. It centers on one good answer and takes responsibility for it. Such thinking could precede a choice of career or the selection of a marriage-partner. It could be at work in the selection of a model for working in physics or analyzing poetry.

The reader will note that my presentation of Perry here in this chapter is primarily a suggestion of the work treated in a more theoretical fashion in Chapters Five and Six. It is as well an indicator that I have chosen to present Perry's work in a formal way at this point in the course.

The formal presentation is followed by a group exercise on the role of women in today's world.[22] The exercise is designed to bring out stereotypical (dualistic) thinking about women and to confront the attitudes of the participants with one

138

another. My own primary purpose in using it is to highlight dualistic thinking among the participants.

At this point in the course I have begun assigning portions of a popular autobiography for the whole class to read. The name of the book I am currently using is *I Know Why the Caged Bird Sings* by Maya Angelou.[23]

At this juncture as well begins our small group work. I ask simply for five examples of dualistic thinking from the first ten chapters of the autobiography named above.

In a typical class of thirty I tell them to arrange themselves in groups of four to six students. I will give them, in this case, half an hour to come up with a consensus statement, signed by all members of each group. I explain briefly some standard strategies for consensus seeking in small groups.[24] The accent on the consensus techniques we are using is on conflict within the group as a tool for deeper understanding. I remind the reader that Kohlberg sees moral development as coming out of situations where conflicting opinions on moral issues are allowed to surface and challenge each other in an ambience of community. Throughout the course we will use the consensus model referred to above, because it lends itself so well to Kohlberg's scheme of moral development.

I teach Perry's whole theory again in the next class, with a new emphasis—the possibility of a cessation of development in Perry's model and the further possibility of regression to dualistic thinking from relativism.[25] There is no built-in development in Perry's model any more than there is in Kohlberg's. The student can turn off the highway of mental development at any stage, and needs to see the patterns of alternatives to growth as a challenge.

We followed the formal presentation with a values clarification exercise called "The Bomb Shelter."[26] In small groups students must decide whom they will allow into a hypothetical bomb shelter in the event of a cataclysmic bomb attack. At the end of the exercise each group reports what they decided and how they decided it. This is my chance to point out examples of dualistic and relativistic thinking. Some groups simply cannot come to any conclusion at all in the allotted time, because they see so many reasons pro and con for letting certain persons share the safety of the shelter. I help them reflect on their thinking, in this case relativistic. The paralyzing power of relativism can come to light in such an exercise. The narrowness of dualistic assumptions can surface also. One group assumed immediately that there would have to be an even number of male and female members in the shelter and made their choices as to whom they would allow in on that unquestioned premise!

Back to the autobiography for the following class. The book is the story of the first sixteen years of the black playwright, actress, poet and dancer Maya Angelou. It is a story of struggle for dignity on the part of a talented young black woman. As Angelou herself puts it:

> The black female is assaulted in her tender years by all those common forces of nature at the same time that she is caught in the tripartite crossfire of masculine prejudice, white illogical hate and black lack of power.
>
> The fact that the adult American Negro female emerges a formidable character is often met with amazement, distaste and even belligerence. It is seldom accepted as an inevitable outcome of the struggle won by the survivors and deserves respect if not enthusiastic acceptance.[27]

I ask the students in groups to give two examples of relativistic thinking in the book. The book itself is written in Ms. Angelou's mature years. Her description of her childhood and adolescence is characterized by committed thinking. Her self-description is thoughtful and wide ranging, but always committed to the dignity of human life. Normally my students try to scratch out some description of her as a relativistic thinker. They know enough to avoid the frequent examples of dualistic prejudice in the book. They find relativism hard to spot and often painfully twist Maya's reflections to show a tinge of relativism. It is a struggle. Discussion after the test

140

reveals the struggle and continues to pose the question "What is relativistic thinking?"

I take the second half of the period to present committed thinking—a formal presentation with questions permitted from the students.

Next class I give a twenty question fill-in test on the whole of the autobiography. The test itself is dualistic by design. When they complete it, I wait for a voice of protest. Finally, timidly, one student objects to my having given such a test. Throughout the remainder of the period discussion gradually builds up. Slowly they realize that they have fallen into a nice dualistic trap called, academically, "the objective test."

Next class, wrapping up William Perry, I spend a half hour summarizing Perry's work. Again, a formal presentation. At the end of this time, we move once more to test.

I show a movie called "A Sense of Purpose"[28] and tell the class that I will show it again at the start of our next meeting, followed by a test asking them to analyze the film in Perry's terms. I want them to be thinking about the movie between classes.

This film is the story of a college basketball player who successfully defies his authoritarian coach. Despite his refusal to play the game the way the coach wants, the team wins the championship. The player isn't sure he wants to continue playing ball. He resists the efforts of a counsellor to convince him to continue. At the end of the film he is being interviewed by the owners of a professional team who try unsuccessfully to intimidate him. We do not know what he is going to do at the film's end. What is clear is that our young man has not decided what sort of person he is going to be. Increasingly he rejects the pat answers of coach, advisor, and future employer in favor of painfully feeling his own way. His thinking is relativistic. My test will reveal whether the class sees this. Here is the test.

1. Simply list three terms we have used thus far in the course that apply to the film you have just seen.
2. Define each of the three terms you have given.

141

3. Use each term in a simple sentence to describe some aspect of the film.

4. Explain why it was that you used each term the way you did in the previous question.

5. A. Choose a part for yourself in the movie. You can choose to be a coach, a parent, a brother or sister, or any other role you want, provided that role allows you to be yourself. Describe that role in a short paragraph.

5. B. What would you say to Hector (the basketball player)? Considering the terms you have used, why did you say it?

The reader will note that this examination is progressive. The first question is mainly concerned with recalling three terms—very likely dualistic thinking, relativistic thinking, and committed thinking. The second question is concerned with the meaning of each of these terms. The third asks the student to apply the terms to the movie. Put concretely, a simple sentence is called for, such as, "The basketball player uses relativistic thinking," or, "The coach in the film is usually dualistic in his thinking."

The fourth question asks for analysis; it desires to know the reasons for which the term was used. A sample good answer: "I stated that the player was a relativist because he sees a number of possibilities for his own future. The use of mere authority is of little help to him. His coach, his counsellor, and the business representatives of a professional team do not impress him with their authoritarian and hence dualistic proposals. He needs to use his own reason as well as time to weigh the proposals."

The last questions asks for synthesis. The student is called to organize in a new way what he or she has learned. The test itself is a step-by-step progression. Each step asks for a more complex form of thinking than the one before it. The progression is taken from Benjamin Bloom's classic work on educational objectives, known popularly as "Bloom's Taxonomy."[29]

I allow the students to work in groups for the first four questions and take an active role in helping those confused by the progressive nature of the questions. The fifth question is the key to the test. The basketball player's thinking is classically relativistic. Authorities from coach to counsellor mean little to him, yet he does not see at all clearly what he is to do. He is struggling for an answer. Many students correctly see the player as relativist. They move from terms right through analysis with ease. However, when they are confronted with "What do you say to Hector?" they often do not have the courage of their own convictions. Frequently they make the question read, "What **advice** would you give to Hector?" It doesn't say that. Still another trap is overlooking the importance of the role they have taken and the circumstances under which they talk to Hector.

In brief, this test is an exercise in uncovering dualism in the students' thinking. It is also meant as an opportunity to take as many factors as possible into account in making their conversation with Hector.

Sample answer to question five: "I am his girlfriend. Hector isn't taking advice these days, so I don't give any. What do I say? 'Hi, Hector! How was the interview with the "pros"?' "

Very few students come up with an answer similar to the one above. One of those who did told me at the end of the course she thought she was going to fail the exam for such a brief answer, but simply could see no other way.

The entire class following this one was spent in a knock-down, drag-out fight between professor and students about the different kinds of dualism they showed in their answers. For some it was the first time they had caught themselves with their own hands in the dualistic cookie jar. Put another way, in the words of one student, "Just memorizing the answers wasn't enough."

We have now spent a considerable part of the course working with cognitive development alone. True, the films, the autobiography, and Perry's final stage of cognitive development are not devoid of ethical issues. The exercises we used all had moral implications and surely involved the students affectively. There was a great deal of empathy elicited by students towards Maya Angelou and Hector the basketball player. Systemic aspects of justice were involved in the world of intercollegiate sport as well as the embattled world of Maya

143

Angelou's struggle to grow up in San Francisco, the black ghetto of St. Louis, and the rural South. We chose, however, to stay for the time, apart from moral concerns. Cognitive development is the backbone of Kohlberg's system, whereas it is rarely a concern of college students. I have been, so to speak, getting them into the ball game via William G. Perry, Jr. We have not been merely watching the game of cognitive development or just learning about it. It has been my goal to have the students see themselves as participators in the game. Now perhaps we are ready for Kohlberg.

2. Engaging the Student in Cognitive-Moral Development

a. Through the Stages Step by Step. We tackle Kohlberg with a formal presentation on my part of Kohlberg's concern for justice, his components and antecedents of moral development, and the meaning of the word "stage." I give each student Kohlberg's own briefest description of his six stages.[30] Each student also receives a brief story about an unpleasant scene in a tavern. Here is the story.

The Way It Was

You were sitting in a bar having a drink with your girl friend. A guy in the booth next to you became obnoxious. He pretends to have known your date from somewhere else, even though she assures both him and you that she has never seen him before. He gets angry when she says she doesn't know him. He's had a few drinks, but is not really drunk. When your lady friend gets up to go to the women's rest room, he makes a grab at her dress and tears it, then gives her a push. She trips, nearly falls, but recovers and disappears into the powder room. That leaves you with a decision to make. What to do? You note that the character in question is about five-feet, six-inches tall, slightly built, and looks sixteen or seventeen years old.

Assume the role of the aggrieved boy friend. What do you do? Why do you do it? Respond in writing.

144

After a short while the students are committed to a course of action which, I trust, involves a dilemma of moral dimensions. Everyone has an answer. The range from a simple "Punch him out" to asking the bartender to quietly remove the offending young man. Some wish to avoid physical beating only because "It's tacky to fight." A considerable but not heated debate arises from the differing opinions, with myself as facilitator-in-chief and head needler.

I explain Kohlberg's stage one after twenty minutes of exchange, pointing out that one could interpret "Punch him out" as stage one justice, assuming something like, "He bothers me; I'm stronger, so I'll nail him."

The next time we meet the class has read Part I of Margaret Craven's short novel, *I Heard the Owl Call My Name*.[31] The book is the story of a young Anglican priest who is sent by his bishop to work as pastor to an Indian village on the Pacific Northwest coast. It is a story of how a young pastor learns the meaning of life and death from his flock. Written in very spare prose, the story is filled with the dilemmas of a people struggling to live in a time of rapid change. The characters in the story run the gamut of Kohlberg's stages in their approach to justice.

I asked each student to pick a character in the book who fits stage one and to explain the reasons for their choices. The choice is not difficult for them. They readily see Sam, a pitiful "rice Christian" type, who beats his wife and his daughter and who lives for the passing pleasure he gets from liquor, as a stage one person. Stage one is familiar territory for my students. They are not stage one people themselves, but each has had to reintegrate his thinking, using this stage as a base, first base, if you will.

After a brief and harmonious discussion of their test answers, I present them with another dilemma. Here is the text.

Who Should Pay

You have been having a great time on a weekend with your boyfriend. Somehow you managed to get a cottage on a lake with privacy. The weather has been beautiful. You have fished, read, and frolicked for two whole days. Just delightful. Sunday is quiet and peaceful. You decide to go into a nice restaurant in a nearby small town for a really good meal to top things off. He pays the bill for dinner. Is it fair to expect that? Why?

Again, the exchange of opinions is friendly. Nobody takes my carefully baited hook. The guy paying for dinner could be paying for sexual services rendered him, but the students don't read it that way—not overtly, anyway. That would be a stage two notion of justice. When I suggest a stage two interpretation, there are some snorts of recognition from some of the women in class. I want the guys to hear those snorts.

The discussion in the main centers around a mixture of what is cool to do to please your boyfriend or what is today's convention. It is a subtle discussion in that it is not all that easy for me to pick up on how they are thinking.

At any rate it leads me into a presentation of Kohlberg's stage two, which takes up the rest of the period. My hope is that we are laying the groundwork for stages three and four where our work will be closer to how they are presently making moral judgments. I do not leave the hard work we have done with William G. Perry behind. Kohlberg's stage one people are demonstrably dualistic thinkers. I try to get the class to see this and will continue to attempt to analyze the kind of thinking going on in each of Kohlberg's stages.

Next class begins with a very brief test on the first three sections of the novel we are reading. Immediately after that I ask them to give me any current slang words that are presently acceptable or "in."

Here is the list that I wrote on the blackboard as the students suggested the words:

cool
swift
heavy

146

far out
tits
super
decent
bad
bomb
gross
zip
loser
yucky
bogue
bummer
drag

I chose the slang list as means to reveal where their values
are. I arranged the words on the board into two categories as
the words came up. One set is complimentary: the other set is
uncomplimentary.

The inference I draw from the words is that the complimentary words are mostly synonyms for the word "cool." The
other list is the opposite of cool. Their slang is indicative of
Kohlberg's stage three. There is great weight placed upon
what pleases important people, "cool," and what does not,
"not cool."

As in the last class, this exercise gives the students an opportunity to observe their way of thinking about their own
values. I want to head off supercilious reminiscences of the
"old days" in junior high school when just about everyone will
admit that their values were dominated by pleasing important
others, in short, by being cool. This is their list of acceptable
words for right now. It gives me my opportunity to explain
formally the characteristics of stage three moral judgments.

In the next class I ask for a brief analysis of a young Indian
girl about to leave her village to marry a white man...the
passage is taken from the book we are reading:

> She was a pretty girl, her hair carefully cut and
> waved, her fingernails red, the heels of her slippers
> very high, and on her face that radiance of

fulfillment, of all the wonders of the new life she was about to enter.[32]

The students like her, and some feel for her. They know that later in the story her man cheats her people out of a precious ceremonial mask, takes her to far away Vancouver, and abandons her there. Completely lost, she dies of an overdose of drugs.

The girl is a study in stage three moral judgment. Her loyalty to her sister is a terrible pull for her to stay at home. Yet she has been swept off her feet by the white stranger. She leaves to please him. He represents the "new way." Her personal loyalty is a tragedy because she has nothing but personal commitment to an unfaithful person to guide her. When the man leaves her in Vancouver, her anchor is gone. She is shattered.

Perhaps she reminds the women in the class of something of the terrible vulnerability of their junior high and high school days. Those were times when most of them were at the mercy of personal loyalty demanded in high school cliques and in-groups. They feel for her. They understand. Their papers show it.

I turn our discussion forward and ask them about the Royal Canadian Mounted Policeman we have seen earlier in the story. What is his notion of justice? He is very much the policeman. It is the law that counts. The students see that, and they also see an undercurrent of thinking that is not as high as the level of the law, an obtuseness and condescension toward the people of the village.

On to a discussion of the law-and-order approach to justice, Kohlberg's stage four. The policeman has already given us a picture of the kind of thinking about justice that sees there must be something more to it than personal loyalty, a larger framework. We see the system of written law for the first time as a basis for justice. It is important to see law's protective power as well as its restrictions. I emphasize this in my presentation.

We finish our presentation of Kohlberg in our next meeting with stages five and six. These are the so-called "principled" stages, characterized by a person's growth into making moral judgments on her own.

I explain the two stages formally and ask the class to work in groups to find characters in the story who represent these two sets of moral development—I set them out in search of the beauty of the old men in the book, the truly principled people. It is a very hard class, because those stages are well beyond most of my students. They see some of the beauty of the old bishop and his friend, the retired missionary, but I have never been able to generate all that much understanding of them in a class of people who are themselves, for the most part, struggling stage-three and four folk in their moral judgments.

We wind up the formal treatment of Kohlberg with a curve ball. I ask them to pick one of two characters central to the book, both young people considering life outside the village in the world of the white man. The students must pick two terms to describe either of these two characters, one from William Perry, Jr. and the other from Kohlberg. The terms must be defined, used in a simple sentence to describe the character chosen. Reasons must be given for the selection of the terms. Finally, the student is to assume a part in the story. As in a previous lengthy test culminating the treatment of Perry's work, they must answer the question "What would you say to the person you have chosen?"

The tricky aspect of the test is this. The two characters they have to choose from are both very winning. Neither is a tragic character. The students are tempted to put them high on Kohlberg's scale, yet each character is in the late teen years. Each is brave to be sure, but their thoughts are somewhere between stages three and four. Both are dualists moving toward relativism.

My students must wrestle with the job of analysis. I am hoping they will realize that real courage and beauty can exist in a human being who has a lot of development still to come.

The students must also assume a role that is believable for themselves and accept that role in a conversation with the character they have chosen and analyzed. This probably means not giving out heavy-handed advice. It will at any rate depend on the kind of person they choose to be and the relationship between themselves and the young Indian. A reasonable conversation will have to take a lot of factors into account. A careful analysis of both one's self and this fictional character must be synthesized into a conversation true to each analysis. As before, I let them work in groups for the first part of the test. The last question, however, they must handle alone.

As in the previous similar exercise, we spent a full period on the test itself and another full period going over the results. The purpose of going over the results? In an atmosphere of community to confront students' moral judgments with something a bit more subtle and integrated than their present thinking.

b. Excursus on Moral Development and the Crisis of Identity. Kohlberg's dilemma. The model for moral development in Lawrence Kohlberg is one of a spiral of ever more integrated thinking about moral dilemmas, assuming a growing ability to empathize with other people. The model does not admit of backward turns. There can be no regression to an earlier way of thinking once you have understood a certain level.

There is a serious problem with this scheme. Young people in the crisis of identity often regress in their moral judgments, as is shown by Kohlberg's own research.[33]

Many of the people in front of me in the classroom are themselves in what Erik Erikson calls the stage of Identity. Oftentimes they have been rather mature young folk previous to this time. Suddenly they become inexplicably dualistic and dogmatic in their thinking, difficult to deal with affectively, and even determinedly irresponsible.

Erik Erikson talks very enlightenedly about this stage of Identity. Although he is a developmentalist, his perspective is different than Kohlberg's. Each of Erikson's stages is a sketch of typical concerns and stresses at given times of life. The stage which Erikson terms the time of Identity is seen as a time of drastic change in one's thinking processes. People in their identity years are seen by Erik Erikson as being typically ideologues, who somehow at the same time haven't really decided where they are going. Because Erikson's sketch of development seems more adequate than Kohlberg's when it comes to describing the thought processes of Identity time, I teach his developmental system at this stage in the course. I am not going through a treatment of how I teach Erikson in a detailed narrative style here, for I have done that in Chapter Four. Suffice it here to say that a presentation of Erikson's work is apt at this point. It should be made in the context of both Perry and Kohlberg. The Socratic method is as important here as it has been elsewhere in the course. I continue to use literature in seeking to bring the matter home. This section of the course comes to its climax and completion in an examination on the character of Holden Caulfield as portrayed by J.D. Salinger in *The Catcher in the Rye*.[34] The full-period exam is like the other two I have described earlier. It is an examination involving an analysis of Holden's character making use of Perry, Kohlberg and Erik Erikson. The final questions, as usual, asks the student to assume a role and talk to Holden in a way consistent with the student's analysis and his or her chosen role.

c. The Model of Elisabeth Kubler-Ross.[35] I finish my course in moral development with the introduction of one further developmentalist, Elisabeth Kubler-Ross. I am not going into a lengthy narration of how I use her work, but am content to give my rationale and a brief look at technique, as I did with my treatment of Erik Erikson.

Kubler-Ross deals with what one might call a person's last chance for development. She works within the period Erik Erikson characterizes as life's last. It is painted by Erikson as a time in which one's life is dominated by the struggle for integrity over the forces of despair.

Kubler-Ross concerns herself with typical patterns of concern on the part of a person at a given period in human life, the period just before death. The pattern of interest in concern typical of a broad time of life makes her work similar to Erikson's, but of course much more narrowly focused. She is vitally concerned with the dying person's **understanding** of

151

what he or she is going through. Hence there are direct parallels with the work of Perry and Kohlberg.

Furthermore, she sees the process of dying as a very rich, if ultimate, time of life, carrying with it a multitude of moral judgments to be made both by the dying person as well as those connected with her by profession, blood, friendship or other bonds.

A study of this ultimate age in life provides the student with abundant opportunity to continue posing moral dilemmas for discussion. I use Kubler-Ross's work then, to summarize and deepen the study of the process of the development of moral judgment. Because she discusses her work in such a readable manner, and because she fills her explanations with so many apt examples, I do not assign reading material outside her book.

The final summation and integration of the matter for the course centers around a film about an old woman dying in a nursing home.[36] It is a fictional story, involving a family's understanding and lack of understanding of the dilemma posed by an old lady's slow death in a nursing home. She is the grandmother once loved and revered, now different and puzzling to her family as she moves closer to death. The students are asked to analyze the old lady's situation, using the vocabulary of all four thinkers we have taken in the course. They are asked to assume a role in the film and speak to the old lady in a manner consistent with both the assumed role and their analysis. This is the final examination for the course.

3. Affective-Volitional Components of Moral Development in the Classroom

Having taken the reader on an excursion through the course itself, I perhaps need not remind him or her that the emphasis has been on thinking. This is very much the Kohlberg approach. Affective and volitional components of moral growth certainly do exist, but they are not the focus of Kohlberg's theory or his educational practice. As he says:

> Stage 6 may be the cognitively most advanced morality, but perhaps those capable of reasoning

that way do not wish to be martyrs like Socrates, Lincoln or King...[37]

My concern as a teacher is to help students develop in making moral judgments. What each student will do with the judgments learned is up to each one. Granted, using literature does engage the affective side of the reader. A good story should have an emotional punch. This is part of the power of literature. It engages a person more wholly than a more abstract approach to theory or a study of cases chosen more for their abstract content than for the power of their presentation. Still, the student is judged by this professor on understanding rather than whether or not he or she does x number of good deeds. I hope for good deeds, it is true, but I sit in judgment only in understanding.

4. Social Role-Taking Components and Antecedents of Moral Development in the Classroom

This third component of Kohlberg's understanding of moral development speaks directly to my use of literature as a vehicle for teaching it. The gifted novelist, playwright, poet or filmmaker has as a primary part of his or her genius the ability to pull the reader or viewer into the story.

I learned years ago that the plays and others works of fiction I loved were the ones in which I was able to identify with one or other of the persons in the story. The characters were believable to me. I felt with them, lived their drama myself; in short, I took their roles. Playing the role of another is not all there is to morality, but it is an essential ingredient. I prefer, then, the work of a gifted humanist in the posing of moral dilemmas to something couched in more scientific terms or in language where the gift of expression is regarded as secondary. I prefer the dilemma of life versus death posed to Hamlet to a more succinct, one-page presentation of a man who must decide whether or not to steal to save his wife's life.

I note further that in my commitment as a teacher to an education that is generalist, I regard it as my job to present dilemmas of morale dimension in the highest artistic form which my students are capable of tackling. My charge concerns the whole of the student mind, not just whatever cranny of it the less-than-inspired prose of social scientists may occupy.

If the narrative portions of this paper have described how I have used literature in teaching moral development, these same portions carry with them a caveat for those sympathetic to this approach. I remind the reader that the books and films here described are carefully tailored to my estimation of what my students' capabilities are, as well as my own range of interest in literature.

For this reason I suggest that each teacher needs to tailor assigned readings to fit both students and himself. A few examples are in order.

Professors in elitist schools could well plunge into Shakespeare, Dostoevsky, Dickens, or Mark Twain, to name four authors I would love to exploit, given a group of precociously literate students.

Teachers in publicly supported colleges, on the other hand, often find themselves dealing with students who have read little. More popular literature is at one and the same time a vehicle for advance in moral judgment and a first acquaintance with serious approaches to letters. Let me suggest some areas for consideration.

Mystery writers are often concerned with justice, from Christie's Miss Marple to Sayers' Lord Peter. P.D. James, among contemporary mystery writers, crafts exceptional English as well as posing very contemporary moral problems.

The lowly Western, with its good guys and bad guys, is nearly invariably concerned with justice being done. Louis L'Amour and Clair Huffaker are representative examples of this concern.

Science Fiction is another vehicle which often finds authors concerned with moral problems in the worlds of the future. In the classics of Aldous Huxley and George Orwell, as well as the more recent works of Isaac Asimov, Arthur C. Clark and Robert Heinlein, there are moral dilemmas galore.

Bernard Malamud and Alexander Sohlzhenitsyn are but two contemporary novelists who pose problems of justice that

I have found apt for my own students. I shall sharpen these reflections by listing briefly the literary works I have myself used in the past five years to pose problems and suggest solutions.

The Autobiography of Malcolm X by Alex Haley. Excellent for seeing moral development and identity crisis, but very long.

The Assistant by Bernard Malamud. The pain of moral growth, the humour, the hope. Beautifully written.

One Day in the Life of Ivan Denisovich by Alexander Solzhenitsyn. Beautiful prose. A variety of moral stages, the suffering of growth.

Nobody Loves a Drunken Indian by Clair Huffaker. Lots of action, moral dimensions of the law.

Brave New World by Aldous Huxley. Chilling presentation of justice not developing.

Huckleberry Finn by Mark Twain. Concern with the law— many examples, especially powerful on religious and racial issues.

Charlotte's Web by E.B. White. Fraught with dilemmas of life and death, faultless prose, far more than a child's book.

I Never Promised You a Rose Garden by Hannah Green. The terror of the struggle to develop, the courage needed.

Cannery Row by John Steinbeck. Steinbeck's shiftless democratic bums as men of principle.

Films. Just to jog the teacher's memory. Fellini and Bergman are passionate and subtle moralists, but difficult. I have never seen, in a more popular vein, a film featuring Jack Nicholson that wasn't filled with moral dilemmas from *Easy Rider* to *Goin' South*. Dustin Hoffman has put his viewers in moral quandaries over the issues posed in many of his films. Of special note are *The Graduate, Midnight Cowboy, Little Big Man* and *Kramer versus Kramer.* Cicely Tyson just doesn't perform unless she is in a role concerned somehow with racial injustice, from *Sounder* to *A Woman Called Moses.*

Television. Just to sample, the moral judgments involved in situation comedies are rife from Archie Bunker to Fred Sanford to the Fonz. The detectives from Kojak to Columbo, from

Rockford to (in his own way) Quincy are all justice seekers of one kind or another.

Poets and singers. Can you forget them? From Robert Burns, e.e. cummings, and Lawrence Ferlinghetti, to name three I have used, stems a treasury of moral conundrums. And there **are** contemporary songs of taste and good craft. I myself look for singers...Roberta Flack, Judy Collins, and Dory Previn have spoken to me. *Both Sides Now,* an old song written by Joni Mitchell, is as good a description of relativistic thinking as I have ever heard.

If I must reluctantly close this whiff of the richness of literature for the moralist, let me do so with comic strips. They are still among the most compact and available of all literatures and most of them are concerned with justice, from the subtleties of Charles Schulz' little people to the grossness of Spiderman...and you don't have to go to the library to get them. Reluctantly, I move on, knowing that each reader must find a list that is personal to him or her and apt to his or her clientele.

5. Systemic Justice Components and Antecedents

If operating actively in a just system is important in moral development, it goes without saying that the classroom itself is a primary system in teaching.

I, for one, have not been successful in devising a means for democratic grading. My grades reflect my judgment, although they can be appealed. I set aside a class period at the end of each semester for such appeals and clarifications.

The establishment of an active sense of community within a class is of paramount importance in teaching moral development. This is why I run more than half of my daily tests in small groups. Students can fight out the answers. Although I do a lot of full-class discussion, still I find that there is more opportunity for opinion interchange in a small group than a big one. An active interchange between students at different moral stages is demanded in Kohlberg's model for moral progression. What Lawrence Kohlberg means by a "just system" is one that is designed to work at the highest possible moral stage. School systems generally operate on a stage four basis, democracies at stage five. My groups are designed to function at stage five, for that reason I set them up on a consensus model. And so, the democratic part of the class takes place in discussion, both in large groups and in small ones.

How the larger structure of the university helps or hinders cognitive-moral development is a subject I choose not to deal with here, although it is surely a worthwhile subject. I have hinted at it in the first chapter of this book.

E. Conclusion and Summary

In seeking closure to this essay, a personal description of Socratic teaching, I shall sum it up. My own approach to teaching cognitive moral development centers around drawing students into discussion in small groups involved with seeking solutions to moral problems posed in literature. Through this discussion it is hoped that they will be challenged to think about the way they make moral judgments and to advance toward moral maturity. Written expression of their views, as well as oral discussion, is demanded. Students are called upon as well to learn and apply not only Kohlberg's system but three other thinkers chosen to cast light on Kohlberg's theory. The hope of this presentation is that it will be an inspiration to originality rather than a course outline for whoever happens to read it. The two chapters following this one are offered in evidence of my own continuing search for better ways to understand and teach human development. They will introduce the reader to a new developmentalist, a man whose work owes much to Kohlberg, Perry and Erikson. His work has struck this observer as opening up new insights to one engaged in studying and teaching moral development. His name is James Fowler.

CHAPTER IX

THE ASYLUM REVISITED

A. Different Views of the Structures of Awareness

1. The University as Asylum

Erik Erikson has said that the chief concern of youth in any age is the finding of something worth being faithful to.[1] My own years of teaching in both high school and college attest to the general truth of Erikson's observation.

For years I have observed undergraduate pilgrimages to one holy grail or another. As I have noted in the opening chapter of this book, one can make a good case for the university campus as a place of asylum and nurture for young people in their search for that special something. The university surely can be a haven for a time of fruitful delay and exploration. It is surely a good place for the gradual shaping of an adult commitment.[2] It is the purpose of this chapter to pick up where Chapter One left off and to examine further the university in its capacity of asylum.

a. Perry and Kohlberg. We have written at length in this book of the research undertaken by William G. Perry, Jr.[3] During the 1950s Perry studied Harvard and Radcliffe undergraduates paying careful attention to their developing intellectual and ethical judgment. There is no doubt that Perry pictures the Harvard campus as a place of intellectual and moral ferment for undergraduates. Intellectual growth typically gave rise to some sort of level-headed and measured commitment on the part of junior and senior students. Harvard is seen as the alma mater, the kind of nourishing institution that Erikson postulates for the advancement of youth to young adulthood.[4]

Lawrence Kohlberg's work, also a chief subject for the essays of this book, provides an ever more rosy glow of optimism for those interested in making a case for the university as a place where a mature sense of moral commitment might be nurtured.[5] Colleges and universities would seem to provide a local habitation for fruitful passages from childhood to adult life.

b. Problems with the Vision. On the other hand, anyone who has nurtured such a view of a university campus could well be called a dreamer. A veneer of rationality does indeed attach to such a vision, but there are holes in the veneer. I am not letting go of the dream, but I find myself increasingly concerned with the holes.

What's to keep a college undergraduate from a fruitful time of passage to adulthood? Erikson's description of the forging of identity seems to fit so well here: "...When each youth must forge for himself some central perspective and direction, some working unity, out of the effective remnants of his childhood and the hopes of his anticipated adulthood..."[6]

(1) Jung's critique. One block that has loomed ever larger in my own vision of the university as a place of asylum is the neglect of the unconscious. I do not mean to say that American higher education is too intellectual, far from it. I do mean to say that most colleges and universities are very rationalistic places. C.J. Jung's comments on contemporary intellectual life seem horribly apropos: "...the marvelous development of science and technics...counter balanced by an appalling lack of wisdom and introspection."[7] Jung's conviction that the unconscious mind "is capable at times of manifesting an intelligence and purposiveness superior to actual conscious insight" is food for thought in a university framework today.[8] In many universities liberal arts are now thrust increasingly into the background in favor of professional programs directly leading to careers in business, engineering or social work, to

160

name three of dozens of professional and pre-professional programs currently offered to undergraduates in my own university. I am not concerned with the evils of studying business, engineering or social work. I am very concerned that scant attention is paid in professional undergraduate programs to insight, intuition, dreams and imagination. This is not a wholly new problem to be sure.

(2) Autobiographical excursus. My own undergraduate education at St. Louis University in the Fifties and Sixties was markedly rationalistic. As a member of the Society of Jesus in training, I received a rigorous formation in Thomistic Aristotelianism. The fact that the younger members of the Order were required as well to study and practice meditation and Christian mysticism puzzled me for years. It was as though there was a tacit agreement to let the unconscious speak in our religious lives and then to never mention it in formal study. We were Augustinian Platonists during the hours of prayer before breakfast and followers of Aristotle and St. Thomas Aquinas for the rest of the day. Rare was the teacher who dared to let one area of our lives talk to the other.

This was a multilinear educational process, the two main strands of which never addressed one another. That we were instructed in a spirtuality that took intuition, prayer and inspiration very seriously preserved us from being thoroughly modern people and kept at least some of us from thinking that we could save the world the way most intellectuals would like to have it saved, by conscious reason alone. I came to regard the lack of dialogue between my mystical tradition and my rational tradition as scandalous and tragic. I felt then as I do now that by and large the rationalists won out.

The mystics remained a suspect but undoubtedly legitimate minority. They were protected by a long tradition of Catholic mysticism. Within this broad tradition was an equally tenacious history of prayer, intuition and imagination going in an unbroken line to Ignatius Loyola, the founder of the Jesuits. His genius in writing the founding constitutions of the Order owes as much to his peculiar intuitive sense and his life of prayer as it does to his Aristotelian Master of Arts degree from the University of Paris.

Well, better to have a bi-linear education than one supported by a single thread! My experience in talking with educators today is that an increasingly large number of them talk only the language of hard-nosed logic, no matter how diversely that logic may be applied to different professional fields.

A weakness of much teaching for any professional goal is that it neglects the powerful underside of a human being called the unconscious.

The voice of the unconscious is difficult to trick out and put to work even with hard labor, but it is nearly impossible to hear if it is denied existence or ignored.

2. Theorists Revisited

a. Kohlberg and Perry Again. If I have seen the university as an asylum for youth in search of identity, I must take a look at the powers and limitations of conscious thought in identity formation. Perry's description of identity formation at Harvard implies an intellectual journey from simplistic black-and-white thinking to sophisticated multi-valent thinking. It is a thought journey in which the typical student begins with simplistic answers for many problems. Throughout the four years of college, the simplicity of the student's thinking is continually challenged to grow in complexity. Students are pushed to consider every intellectual problem in its context. They learn to think in terms of figure and ground, in accordance with each situation, taking into account all the circumstances in which any individual problem may occur in the gamut of learning—from hard science to literature. Their thought processes become more nuanced. In fact, most of Perry's subjects become sophisticated to a point where they came to think that there was no final answer for any problem. All answers and solutions were typically considered to be relative, situational, temporary. From this state of sophisticated uncertainty, Perry finds a progression to what he calls "committed thinking." Committed thinking is not an abandonment of contextual and measured thinking. It is a going beyond it. By a leap of faith, the typical Harvard undergraduate did make career choices, church commitments, marriage commitments, going well beyond the welter of indecisiveness attendant upon his nuanced intellectual skills. The study points up the need for genuine commitment on the part of educated youth, but it does not underline or explore sufficiently the source of such commitment. The indication is that subtle conscious thinking will lead inevitably to a source of identity and the making of important choices.

Kohlberg's studies of moral development trace a line of growth even more dependent on conscious thought alone than Perry's. Kohlberg's fine work on growth in moral maturity by his own admission is dependent upon the subject's rational and conscious development. The unconscious as a source of human growth is simply not of concern in Kohlberg's work.

Although he pays tribute to Erikson's analysis of Identity, Kohlberg seems to this observer to overlook Erikson's concern, typical of the psychoanalyst, for both conscious and unconscious factors in human development. Erikson's description of the path from childhood to adulthood is one that surely pays much attention to unconscious factors. How telling is his quotation from William James as regards to the way a person's character (read Identity) comes clear:

> A man's character is discernible in the mental or moral attitudes in which, when it came upon him, he felt himself most deeply and intensely active and alive. At such moments, there is a voice inside which speaks and says: "This is the real me!"[9]

How closely this parallels Jung's description[10] of a person's inner voice in a dream, a voice he identifies as that of the unconscious, superior in intelligence and purposiveness to the conscious insight. It is not possessed by a person in the same way as one's conscious voice, but has a kind of independence, a life, as it were, of its own.

Whatever the source of this authoritative voice, hidden often from one's self except in rare moments of intuition and in our dreams, it is a voice to be taken very seriously. For Erikson, it is a voice "that comes upon him," hence somehow

163

elusive and possessed of a life of its own. It is the very voice signalling one's identity. It is precisely not the voice of logic, but something else.

I find many of today's educators concerned with cognitional and ethical development treating this voice with less than respect. I have used Kohlberg and Perry as examples of this rationalism, but perhaps there is a far heavier weight attached to the sad plight of liberal arts education in this country and the switch to college programs focussing primarily and nearly exclusively on what the nursery rhyme has summarized as "doctor, lawyer, merchant, chief."

If one is to understand today's undergraduates, I assert that we must understand their unconscious intellects as well as their conscious ones. If we are to teach them, we must teach to both aspects of the mind.

It is not my purpose here to go into detail as to how one can teach mathematics, physics or business with emphasis on the unconscious mind. I nevertheless submit that a mathematician, physicist or business person without intuition or imagination will be capable of dealing with only the most rudimentary problems of his or her profession. A course in English literature leaving behind inspiration becomes sterile. Historians and social scientists, if they wish to avoid mere reviewing "the facts" or generating huge amounts of useless empirical data, need to be in touch with their own unconscious minds. Psychology, above all, needs recognition of the unconscious if it is not to betray its study of the human psyche.

b. The Issue of Identity. I feel it necessary to underline here a basic issue concerning youth's search for knowledge, an issue which is raised at the beginning of this essay and fundamental to the essay's progression. What the undergraduate wants most to know is none other than himself. He or she searches for the answer to the question "What have I got, and what am I going to do with it?"[11] A good answer to this question, or the beginning of such an answer, undergirds all disciplinary areas of knowledge. It is basic to this presentation that as a student learns competence in one or various areas of knowledge during

164

the college years, the search for identity goes on concomitantly. The two endeavors interpenetrate one another. If one can make a case for utilizing what one might call the submerged part of the mind as a part of competence in any academic field, the case for sensitivity to the unconscious mind goes double in the search for identity.

Perry and Kohlberg both see the way a student thinks as related to the quest for identity.[12] Intellectual development is vital to identity development in the work of both. The bias toward the unconscious in the work of both Erikson and Jung has brought this author to see the limitations of Perry and Kohlberg's work. We need empirical data concerned with knowing in a less rationalistic sense in order better to understand the patterns of thinking in students as they grow towards identity and beyond it. Such data is now coming forth.

c. James Fowler's Contribution. Since 1972, a researcher named James Fowler has been interviewing people concerning how they understand their worlds.[13] Like both Kohlberg and Perry, Fowler is a developmentalist. He is consciously in debt to Kohlberg and Erikson and familiar with Perry.[14] His concern with structures of knowing is broader than Kohlberg's and Perry's. Fowler's understanding of the way a person knows includes intuition and imagination, so characteristic in Jung's theory. It includes an element of trust, so important a factor in Erikson. It includes as well the whole area of logic and conscious thought so prominent in the studies of Kohlberg and Perry.

Speaking of the kind of knowing which concerns him, Fowler says: "It is a knowing or construing in which **cognition** (the 'rational') is inextricably intertwined with **affectivity** or **valuing** (the 'passional')...one trusts, or fears, resents, distrusts, and revolts against."[15]

This notion of knowing is a very rich one. It speaks to the overarching search for something worthy of fidelity, to the quest for identity, to the need for discovering what I stand for. The developmental patterns in which such a notion of knowing typically progress can be of great value to the teacher or

165

professor engaged in meeting the student on the two-fold ground of academic learning and self-discovery.

B. A Teacher's Reflections on James Fowler—Step by Step through the Stages

If I have presented James Fowler's model for cognitional development as a good one for understanding undergraduates, indeed a good model for understanding students on any level, my presentation has admittedly remained abstract. I want now to come down to cases. How can Fowler's theory be put to work in the world of formal schooling? I must warn the reader that James Fowler has studied "knowing" in a wide range of people from children to old folks. And so, although the chief focus of this paper remains undergraduates in college. I am going to comment on teaching in the light of each of Fowler's stages, from first to last. I do this partly to help the reader see the scope of Fowler's work and partly because it is my opinion that you can understand teaching any given student better if you know what the student's ways of learning once were and what they are likely to develop into.

I want the reader to note that Fowler is a developmental structuralist. He is concerned with how people know things rather than what they know. In other words, he is concerned with the structures of knowing. As a developmental structuralist, he is concerned with patterns of understanding that grow in a regular sequence. These patterns of understanding he calls "stages." The typical way in which one stage yields to another is invariant in order and allows no skipping. Hence we find a progression in ways of knowing that is predictable. I shall present the stages in the order in which Fowler has found them to occur. I will comment on each stage from the point of view of the teacher.

I shall attempt to point out the strengths of each stage in the knowing process with the goal of providing the teacher (or the student) with a sort of teaching map, a guideline to typical learning strengths in the student. The presumption is, of course, that the teacher best presents the matter to be learned in a way comprehensible to the student. The structures in which the student knows and makes sense of his world should have a lot to do with how I teach him. I want to teach to the strength of the student.

1. The Stages

Stage One

James Fowler's first stage of knowing usually occurs in children between the ages of four and seven years of age. We normally will find children of this stage in kindergarten and the first two grades of primary school. Children at this stage understand the world about them as fluid and filled with novelty. They have a very deep sense of wonder about the world, born partly because of the world's newness to them. They have as yet little understanding of cause and effect. Their world is a small one dominated by family figures with whom lies their basic sense of trust.

A teacher of small children, whether a parent or other, should capitalize on the child's sense of wonder. "Show and tell" is important for kindergartners. Fairy stories involving marvelous and magic events, stories of religious wonders, music, painting—all these activities will speak to the focus of those young poets.

Stage Two

If a child at stage one can be called a poet, what's the progression to another way of knowing the world? The stage one children see their world as though it were a series of beautiful and sometimes terrifying pictures, each one separate from another. Then comes the discovery of connections. Somewhere during the years six to twelve children start putting order in things. They put order in words—and so they love to listen to and to tell stories. They are concerned with simple sequences of cause and effect, which takes some of the magic out of their world and puts some order in it. They can put order in numbers as well as words, hence simple arithmetic functions are possible for them to understand. Given the push, they will write stories, narrative folk that they are. Their deepest knowing, their values, their trusted ones, will appear in narrative form. Teachers and parents should capitalize on this gift of narration. Abstract reasoning still counts for little. One can see everything that these folks know as a line of narrative. One can count on them to want to put everything in a basic, linear order. It is to this linear strength that the teacher should address himself.

As our narrative people put their world in a neat and linear order, it should not surprise us if they become lawyers, i.e., they become very interested in rules. You don't know primary school children until you hear them arguing about the rules— of street ball, Monopoly, crazy eights, hopscotch, or even arithmetic.

A happy child in primary school is one who can master and keep at least a portion of the rules. They'll love spelling and arithmetic if they can keep the rules. They are devastated if they cannot. A teacher must have clear rules and reams of things to be ordered, to work with the strength of these children.

Stage Three
And so the onslaught of puberty and a new kind of reasoning which can handle abstractions and look beneath the surface to a person's intentions. Yesterday's narrators and lawyers have become today's personalists. They are concerned for each other's intentions in keeping rules. This is a time for new levels of friendship, a time for crushes.

A teacher can count on an audience for literature that features friendship, nobility and idealism—anything that involves one-to-one companionship. Inspiration is a key.

Let it be known, of course, the inspiring persons and uplifting stories must be conventional. Teenagers are very conservative people. Their understanding of friendship and loyalty, for all its depth, has not progressed very far. Loyalty to friends begins with imitation. One shows loyalty to a friend or small group by an unthinking imitation of the most trivial behavior of that group—from shoes to hair styles, there is a code, a uniform.

A teacher would do well to realize how strong is the need for students of this stage to conform to the wishes of their friends. A successful teacher will regard the clannishness of students at this stage as a strength to be utilized rather than just a kind of millstone around the student's neck. Many a teacher has despaired of getting students to study because study was not the "in" thing in such-and-such a clique of young people. I am suggesting active probing on the part of the teacher to harness their focus on friends' activities rather than trying to wish it away.

If one version of this stage is characterized by conformity to friends, there is a progression beyond this that is still a part of this pattern. This progression is characterized by the discovery of law. It is just as conventional as the friendship stage, for it no more questions law than it earlier questioned the facts of friendship. Still, it is a way of knowing that discovers the value of a fixed order in things. A teacher could very likely speak to this discovery of law and order beyond friendship in the world of mathematics and science. At a later stage of development, a student might see that science is not so orderly as first he or she thought, but right now the dizzying order and beauty of science and math can be a powerful inspiration to a student who is discovering a world of law beyond small groups of friends.

I note further that this stage has adult as well as teenaged versions. Some young adults who are undergraduates in college and some older people continue to build their lives around interpersonal values and being cool, or the inviolability of the law. These people tend to be subtler than their high school counterparts, not quite so obvious in their conformity to friends or law, but they do present the same strengths and weaknesses to a teacher. Perhaps what is important for the teacher is not to presume that this stage has only high school representatives. Colleges are loaded with people who put their world together in this pattern.

Stage Four

Picture a student who is manufacturing his or her own world view, moving away from significant others for a view of

169

the world. Picture a student standing alone and apart from others, aware of being alone, aware of being apart. Picture a student who has mastered contextual thinking. This is a person at least twenty years old but possibly thirty or even forty. She knows as well that other people have different legitimate ways of looking at life, but she typically and generally unconsciously reduces other folk's ways to her own categories and hence is less open to others than she realizes.

Where do you find such a student? There are always some upper-class undergraduates with such a profile. In graduate school there are more. In my own experience with older undergraduate students, often women in their thirties and forties, this stage is prominent.

What are the strengths of such a student on which a teacher might focus? There is a certain, almost defensive independence. A student will have a world-view wider than family and friends, and for the first time be critical of the laws of church and state that have seemed so unquestionable in the immediate past. Such a student can question the underpinnings of any body of knowledge. He or she is capable of personal synthesis of knowledge. One could call such a person a philosopher capable of picking and choosing a world view from a wide variety of sources. If this student is a bit of an ideologue, often condescending to those who see life differently, the teacher might well reflect that there seems to be no path to a reasonable and responsible nuanced way of knowing the world that bypasses such a painful period of putting on airs. Erik Erikson writes with great empathy about snobbish ideologues with new-found identities.[16] To have a world view still a little simpler than the world is the mark of a hard-won battle for wisdom, a battle as yet very much in progress. It becomes easier for a professor to bear with the intellectual snobbery of a student if the professor sees that snobbery as a stepping-stone to tolerance.

Stage Five

And where does a student typically go from a period of rather defensive and lonely synthesis we have just seen? Most of them go away! There are few students still engaged in formal schooling older than thirty years of age. This stage is a mid-life development, if it occurs at all. It is rare among students.

We can characterize it as a sort of second childhood wherein the world becomes again numinous, wonderful and seductive. It is a stage of knowing that is much less given to drawing lines of demarcation in one's view of the world. Persons of the previous stage have their world together all right, but they tend to resemble porcupines. They are well defended and often unknowingly defensive. The stage under discussion is more like a sponge than a porcupine. It is characterized by opening one's way of knowing, letting down one's guard. It is more accepting. It takes into account, often for the first time, not only conscious messages of wider horizon than heretofore, but unconscious elements as well. It is characterized by turning in on one's self and back in one's history as well as foraging in new pastures outside the self and looking to the future.

For the first time we see real tolerance, for the first time real breadth. The structures of most university graduate programs are not aimed at satisfying folks of this stamp. In a sense, there is little use to speak of them as students due to their rarity. We can, however, speak of such people as professors.

A description may help. Such professors no longer owe allegiance to a single field of learning. They tend to look puzzled when asked "What is your field?" or "What do you teach?" They are not wedded to a given academic discipline and tend to be bored by squabbles as to whether Humanities or Social Science or Science has the "correct methodology" or the final answer. They are not given to exclusive religious affiliation anymore than they are tied to one department of learning. They are people capable of sticking their noses into any intellectual pie, any religion or philosophy, with interest as well as the conscious risk of conversion. Let us call these people generalists; less romantically, we can call them "retreads."

Their value in the world of academe for teaching is inestimable, because they can take a student in the student's own niche and accept him there. They can encourage young physicists in their physics, poets in their poetry, business persons in their business. They can find interest and enthusiasm in most intellectual fields, many religious and philosophical areas. These teachers can nurture learning of all kinds in students. They can understand youthful enthusiasm without being put off by its inevitable ideological content. The person who takes all thought seriously, if he or she is a rarity among students, should not be a rarity among professors.

I hasten to add that I do not mean to exclude the enthusiasm of youth from the teaching profession. There is surely a place for young teachers of narrower scope. Enthusiasm and energy are among the pearls of great price in teaching; they take an especially vibrant form in the youthful teacher. No matter that young men and women just coming from graduate school are not so tolerant as they themselves believe. They are still a chief means for updating and challenging their older colleagues who may be broader in their intellectual perspective, but also more likely lazier. "A body at rest tends to remain at rest," as every professor knows.

Stage Six

There is a last stage of knowing, which intelligence might require me to leave out of a study of teachers and students, since to my experience, there are no students at all of any formal level in this category. I can admit to never having had a professor actively engaged in teaching here either. What is this exalted height?

A person whose making sense of the world and whose approach to knowledge falls in this pattern is a very rare bird indeed.[17] If you can imagine someone as open to different ways of knowing as in the previous stage, but differing markedly from the previous pattern in that he or she has become at home with such a way of knowing, you'd be close to the mark. Typical subjects in the previous stage were spongelike individuals, but generally pulled and torn by the inevitable paradox of taking contradictory ways of knowing seriously. There is a built-in vulnerability in the removal of

172

one's intellectual defenses. There is often a longing for simpler days, for earlier years when one was blessed with certainty.

The individual who has surpassed such a tendency to looking back, the person who no longer feels such a deep sense of paradox in the ways of knowing, this is the person of whom we speak. There is a simplicity here, a sense of travelling light, a sense of unity with the world, rendering one beyond the cares of householding and generating. There is a sense of being above the turmoil, a readiness to suffer death, large or small. One associates this time in life with old age, with retirement, with a cessation of ambition.

Is there anyone in any way associated with academe functioning at this level? Surely many persons with such freedom as we have described would be looked at askance by large and generally conservative organizations. Almost all the historical personages James Fowler lists at this stage, from Gandhi to Martin Luther King, Jr., died violent deaths related to their lack of orthodoxy.[18] The list is an indication of how well such folk are accepted by humankind at large.

The one or two teachers I have met who seemed as above it all as this pattern would indicate were near retirement age or past it. I should note that these folk often take on protective coloration due to their lack of personal ambition. It may well be that a university community frequently has an emeritus professor quite content with the obscurity of retirement, known to a few people and having a great influence on those few. The world has passed this person by. Perhaps she was once well known for a discovery, years of productive scholarship or intellectual innovation, but is now out of the public eye in her years of wisdom. I think of Dorothy Day in her eighties living on a farm in New York or the paleontologist-theologian Pierre Teilhard de Chardin's last years living in an obscure apartment in New York City.

There is something about these people that puts them beyond institutions. I don't want to say there are no professors among them, just that I think they would likely be hard to find as profs. If you really don't need to be noticed, you probably won't be in the papers or featured on "Sixty

Minutes." To benefit from the privilege of having such a person for a teacher would require unusual perspicacity on the part of the students themselves.

2. View from the Top

a. Passages. So much for an overview. Are there things one might now observe having ranged through Fowler's six stages? I believe so. Certainly one issue that should come to any teacher's mind is the question of passages. I shall define a passage briefly as a time when one is in transition, moving from one pattern to another. I have not found extensive documentation in Fowler's work as to the characteristics of passage. He notes that older people moving from stage three (loosely termed "interpersonal") to the next more independent stage find this time frequently to be a breakup as well as a breakthrough. If transition is not given extensive treatment by Fowler, we can note that he is quite definite that his stages are "structured wholes."[19] They are periods of integration. Generally speaking, when a person moves from one integrated way of putting one's world together, there is a time of disintegration and pain. Erik Erikson speaks very beautifully of such a passage in his work on the crisis of Identity. Speaking of the word "crisis" he says that the word "no longer connotes impending catastrophe, which at one time seemed to be an obstacle to the understanding of this term. It is now being accepted as designating a necessary turning point, a crucial moment, when development must move one way or another, marshalling resources of growth, recovery, and further differentiation."[20]

It goes without saying that any teacher will find some students whose ways of knowing are more characterized by disequilibrium than equilibrium. For a teacher herself to regard her work as connected vitally with provoking passages and crises in the student lies close to what learning is all about. The developmental point of view does not look upon the pain of passage as something pathological. It may hurt, but it doesn't mean you're crazy. Passages are precisely perilous paths to new equilibrium. They are a part of growth to be moved into.

174

They are not signs of disease or decay to be "remedied" or patched up.

And so, the teacher is seen as working two ways. The first way I have described throughout much of this essay. It is the way of identifying patterns of strength in a student and teaching to those patterns. The second way is the way of the gadfly. If I can provoke a student towards a more complex way of putting his world together, I will do so, with full knowledge that there will be a painful passage, a time of disintegration, accompanying the change.

At this point, perhaps the reader will be beginning to grow tired of a paper which is meant to open new perspectives on teaching or at least provide new structures for old perspectives. "Is this treatment ever going to get practical?" you ask. I shall reply that if not practical, it can at least admit some practical problems.

b. Mixture of Stages. What, for example, does a teacher do in a class in which there is a lovely mix of stages and passages from one stage to another? One answer, of course, is to say that teachers have always had the problem of different kinds of students in one room. It is of interest to me to find identifiable patterns in my students. I rarely find college undergraduates in more than two of Fowler's stages—stages three and four, with lots positioned in between. I challenge my personalists to begin moving into the uncharted and wider waters of stage four. I encourage those who are on their way—and I make use of my cactus-like independents who are at stage four to continue to put their new found critical tools to work. This is a big job, of course, but I do have a pattern to work on which gives my teaching a direction, a focus, even a boldness.

c. Conscious vs. Unconscious. Another question a reflective reader might come up with might concern the issue of conscious vs. unconscious, raised so passionately early in this paper and then seemingly dropped. With the overview the reader now has, perhaps he could identify certain stages likely to be open to the intuitive side of the self. I would

175

unhesitatingly pick stages one, three and five as times in life especially open to the dark world, the rich world of the unconscious. A teacher should know that there are mystic times in the life cycle—and teach to them. By the same token, there surely are stages when logic and conscious thought are apt tools to a student.

I do not mean, of course, that any teachers should ever abandon the hard world of logic in the classroom. I submit, however, that my still sharp-edged and numinous memory of the joy of climbing into a locomotive cab as a kindergartener is a reminder to me that similar terrifying holy adventures are apt for other students when their poetic, intuitive and mystical side surfaces again, later in life, in a regularly recurring cycle.

C. Conclusion

And so, a presentation of the student as one engaged in a rich and cyclic pattern of growth, now intuitive, now logical, ever increasing in complexity. A presentation of a student, much of whose pain is the pain that comes from moving from one pattern of knowing the world to another. The pain of growth rather than decay. The teacher as one who teaches to strengths and capabilities in students as she sees them in a developmental structure. A teacher who acts as a goad, needling and pushing students to the abyss of disequilibrium because she thinks that abyss leads somewhere. And finally, the teacher as an artist who attempts to bring students in various stages of development into fruitful contact with each other and their subject matter all in the same classroom. If this essay has stirred its readers to more questions than answers, more puzzles than pat solutions, its author will rest and be pleased, in a rare moment of equilibrium himself.

It is with the hope that the reader's curiosity concerning James Fowler's stages has been aroused that I offer a different look at Fowler in the next and last chapter of this book. The presentation there is not concerned directly with the classroom. It might be called a poet's presentation of Fowler's stages. It is certainly autobiographical. It owes as much in its conception of Fowler's work to insight and imagination as it does to hard logic. Let us then proceed....

176

CHAPTER X

A SEQUENTIAL SEXTET: Portraits of Faith Stages in One Family

A. Introduction

1. One Family

The heart of this chapter is a description of the faith of six different people. The first description is one of a six-year-old child. The last concerns the final months of a terminally ill woman of seventy-five. The studies are of real people. They are members of the same family group, spanning three generations. If my stated concern is to study the faith of each of these people, that in itself needs some explaining. It should come as no surprise to the reader of the previous chapter that faith in the present one is seen from the theoretical vantage point of a way of knowing. The model is that of James W. Fowler.[1] The richness and attractiveness of Fowler's model to one engaged in teaching was the point of the chapter preceding this one.

2. Faith Defined by Fowler

It is not my intent here to defend Dr. Fowler's structural and developmental approach to patterns of faith. Rather I propose to use Fowler's theory to shed light on my own observations of a single family. If my six portraits speak to the reader with enough vigor to arouse curiosity, then he or she can read Fowler himself.

Let us begin with the notion of faith. Fowler does not regard faith as something that one has, like money in the bank or a head of hair. It is not so much an attribute as it is a way of doing something.[2] We are talking about a way of **knowing** something. Fowler sees knowing as a unique process for each person, and yet he finds in his research sequential patterns of knowing among people. He is not the first to do this of course.

a. Fowler's Debt to Piaget, Kohlberg, Erikson. For nearly the past fifty years Jean Piaget has been studying how people know, finding patterns of knowing among children, patterns that change and become more complex as they grow older in their active experience of the world around them.[3] Jean Piaget's experimental studies have helped the world to understand that kids are not just small grownups. They think differently, and their patterns of thinking are constantly developing.

Lawrence Kohlberg is another developmentalist who is concerned with thinking.[4] His primary concern is how people develop in their thinking about right and wrong. Like Piaget's, his studies reveal an invariant **sequence** in the way people develop moral judgment.

Erik H. Erikson is a third developmental thinker whose work is at the roots of Fowler's synthesis on faith.[5] Erikson has for fifty years studied typical patterns of concern at different periods of human life, from birth until the period of life preceding death in old age.

b. Faith Stages. Fowler has made use of all these thinkers in his interviews with people about faith.[6] He has a theory which posits six stages of faith. In his model these stages must follow one another without skipping. After the first, any one of the six stages may be final. There is no guarantee that any one will progress from stage one through stage six. There is a progression, but Fowler himself is at pains to say that he himself does not believe that the last stage should be a goal to strive for. He refuses to enter into debate as to which stage is better.[7] He is more concerned with diagnosis than he is with prescribing a path to perfection.

c. The Object of Faith. We have digressed from the subject of faith's meaning. So far we have seen that our professor sees it as an action word. The action is taken to be one way of knowing. Knowing what? Watch now; Fowler does not say that faith is a way of knowing God. He calls the object of this kind of knowledge the "ultimate environment."[8] For most of us that term itself needs explaining. He also calls the object of faith "those sources of power and values not subject of human control."[9]

Let's work on that. For most individuals who believe in God, we assume that God is the "ultimate environment." God, he or she, is the final source of power beyond my personal control. I note, however, that there are those who regard the collective human race as the ultimate source of power in the cosmos. I note further that it might well be possible to regard General Motors, the Internal Revenue Service or the United States of America as the ultimate environment or the source of power and value beyond my personal control.

Our theory doesn't dig into what God or Ultimate I have my faith in, but rather how I do the deed.[10] Our model of faith then not only cuts across denominational lines of definitions of God, it goes further. One does not have to be a "believer" to indulge in the activity Fowler calls "faithing." The structure of the way I know what or whomever I endow with ultimate power has a discernible pattern, a regular series of steps in growth that is basic to being a human being, whether one is religious or not.[11]

A word on the activity of knowing. My thoughtful reader will be aware that there are lots of ways of knowing things and people. I can know my times tables as a third grader, but that's quite different from the way I know my Mom or my younger brother.

We are talking about the activity of knowing in a very rich sense—much more like knowing my Mom than like knowing my times tables. When people know people, that activity is not just cold intellectual measurement. The way I know you involves my feelings as well as my various intellectual capacities. When I talk knowing the "ultimate environment" or "the source of power and value beyond my control," inevitably I involve an attitude toward the community of persons around me in my vision, my personal philosophy. I think you could do worse in getting an initial line on this "knowing" than to say it's the **way** I put together my philosophy of life. As Fowler puts it:

> Faith is an active mode of being-in-relation to another or others in which we invest commitment, belief, love, risk and hope.[12]

We are talking about progressive styles of life philosophizing, each step building on the last, and going beyond it. There is more, much more, to be said of this form of stage theory. The point of this essay, however, is to present a family in six stages of faith development, as I have observed them, off and on, over a lifetime. I shall let the reader pick the threads of development from my sketches. I mean to challenge the reader to see if these portraits ring true. If they do, there is the further challenge of the empirical work of Fowler itself. Do the sketches confirm, deny, or add life to Fowler's work? That's a question the reader will have to answer.

I am aware that the reader may want some brief description of each stage taken separately. For this reason I have put a note at the title of each of my six characterizations. The note will briefly describe the characteristics of the stage concretely embodied in the main body of the text. And so we begin.

B. The Family O'Connell

1. Matthew at Six

Fowler calls the first of his stages "intuitive-projective." It is characterized by imitation of powerful and primal adults. There is little differentiation between fantasy and fact. Stories, imaginations, characters in any medium of literature, from television to family reading, are seen as real. There is a sense of wonder for ordinary things, but little capacity to see the necessity of having causes for effects. The world is magical, capricious, and frightening as well as marvelous.

Matthew and I spend long hours together. We do housework. We make shelving for the family apartment. We cook together, eat together, read aloud together. He is a six- year-old boy and I am his father. This year I am working at home

180

and taking a large part of the householding duties of our family.

Two nights ago he woke up and got dressed, because he thought it was morning. I was watching an old Henry Fonda western on TV. He stayed with me, in the big chair, sitting in my lap with the dark room around us. We sipped a glass of bock beer and ate saltines while watching Fonda knock off the bad guys for the last half hour of the movie. Gently then, I got him back to bed. We do a lot of things like that. Matt's human world is still pretty small, slowly growing as he wends his way through the first grade here in Atlanta, but small nonetheless. His ultimate authorities are few, just a couple of us. He startled me the other day when we were working with an electric drill making lead holes for screwing together a wooden step ladder. "Dad," he said, "you are some kind of a carpenter."

Matt doesn't spend all his time with me. Anything he can see is interesting. He draws pictures with crayons, of spacemen, flowers, trees. One of his pictures shows him alone at his grandmother's grave, crying. A caption says, "I want my mommy." His world is one of great wonder, but it is a capricious world in which anything can happen any time. Matt understands little about causes. Things just happen. He's afraid his mother might just disappear the way his grandmother did. His whole consciousness is one of small and intense bites into life. He is a poet, but not a narrative poet. He is a seer. I think it would be silly to talk about God or ultimates very much to him as something separate or beyond his world. His whole world is charged with short episodes of wonder. In religious terms, everything is numinous to him. No grownup need explain that to him, only to recognize it.

He likes me to call him "Matthew Fishing O'Connell," because that name recognizes him as a person and reminds us both of that blinding moment when he pulled a malevolent looking catfish from the dark waters of Asylum Lake last spring. That was an experience of the Ultimate!

He is not often lonely, as long as he has it in the back of his head that his mother and I do exist and are not about to be snatched away from him by a capricious "ultimate power" who might just wander out of the television set and take one or the other of us to another planet.

I have said he works with me. Well, we work together, sometimes on the same project, but we are parallel lines. We are close, but each does something rather separate. Matt's friends are interesting creatures with whom he finds it pleasant to play his game. He is concerned that they be present, but not too much so. He is no philanthropist.

What are the challenges to this small boy's trust-knowing of the world? He must deal with the possibility of death or loss without the benefit of knowing how either is caused. He likes lighting candles in church, because the flame stays lit all week. Somehow a source of faith/knowing now and for the future is his sense of utter wonder at ordinary things, and the residue of the steady presence of myself and his mother.

2. Joe at Eight

This second stage is termed by Fowler "mythic-literal." The person widens the area of faithing beyond the primal adults of stage one to the wider community of neighborhood, friends and school. This way of knowing expropriates available symbols, stories, and manners as forms of faithing and takes them literally.

Joe is another small boy, but how much different is his third-grade world from his brother's. Joe has a lot more bosses. He's gone wide screen on us, like a movie as compared to a TV set . He knows teachers. He reads books. He's a member, not only of a school class, the Cub Scouts, and the apartment urchins; he even has cousins in St. Louis!

Joe likes stories—long ones, from *Tom Sawyer* to *The Hobbit*. The heroes of those stories are very real to him, not quite so real as to threaten snatching him up to another land right from the printed page, but real enough for him to like them and fear them. Joe doesn't just go to church; he has his favorite priests, if you please. Did I forget John Travolta, Johnny Bench, and the Incredible Hulk? Joe's face is like that

of a small rodent—alert, testing the air, twitching, nosey. He
has a lot of people to please.

How does he weigh his new-found multitude? Which of
them carry the most weight? He has affinities for folks. Some
people just fit, like Father Fred Kammer, who can juggle
three tennis balls, and even **tried** a soccer ball and two soft-
balls in our living room after dinner one night. His mother's
consistent love impresses him most. He counts on her. And
then there's his **competent** group. I head that list...he's learning about the importance of competency at school. He has
orthodox friends too, people who know the rules and keep
them. What a God he has! Right out of *Star Wars,* I think. His
God can **do** things, but must do them correctly, consistently,
and with pizazz.

Joe's twitchy nose has a foraging mind behind it, a mind
that can follow a long adventure, ask about causes, make
endless lists—"collections" he calls them—of bottle caps,
baseball cards, old spark plugs, words from the dictionary.
Did you ever think how many different ways you can order six
hundred and seventy-three baseball cards? You can do it
according to team, position, batting averages, All-Stars,
rookies—I'm just scratching the surface. You can argue
endlessly over games you play with cards too. For rules are important. And Joe knows they should be kept.

Joe's games are more cooperative than his brother's. Other
folks **do** have an existence. He might even defend a close
friend. Joe feels for those who get a raw deal. It is very clear to
him in his stories that there are bad guys and good guys. When
I asked him why he defended a smaller friend in a fight, he
said it simply, "That other boy was mean!"—so Joe hit him as
hard as he could—and Joe is an honorable man.

And for my inquisitive moralist, what are the sources of his
faith? He needs order in his world, his schoolwork has led him
to "honest method." He needs to see it in the way the world
works and in the way it treats him. He pushes his search for
method and cause to his God and his fate. He does indeed still
find his world a capricious place. I think of the bewilderment
of his anger when he skins a knee skateboarding. It doesn't

seem fair! Still, he invests deeply in his "good guys" for a sense of worth, for his rock-bottom view of the world that stretches out on his new wide screen. That larger scale is his challenge.

3. "The Oaf" at Seventeen

"Synthetic-conventional" faith. Real loyalty to individuals is possible at this stage. Faith is beginning to make sense out of a widely differentiated set of groups outside the family. This synthesizing takes place according to the conventions that stem from individual loyalties.

John was known to his intimates as "The Oaf," intimating perhaps that unlike Joe and Matthew he had no overseer, no boss or authority outside himself. Not so, even if he was at great pains to make it seem that way. The Oaf's authorities were very personally scrutinized by himself before he accepted them, but once found acceptable or inevitable, they were dictators. He was the ninth of twelve children, with five talented older brothers, not to mention two quick younger ones. I don't know when he began to play the clown, but I do know that he learned the role in earnest in his late high school years. He had a vast number of personal calling cards printed up for himself with John "Oaf" O'Connell emblazoned on them for all the world to see. His friends, brothers, sisters, and schoolmates helped keep him in that role. It allowed him to exist as one different than the talented multitude of his siblings, parents, cousins and other encroachers on his personhood, but it was an uncomfortable and degrading position. He was helped by a powerful aunt's backing in escaping a disastrous boxing career, imposed upon him by imposing and authoritative brothers and cousins. Soon after, he took up music, which was acceptable, because other older cousins played "country music." In our family obviously, older cousins could be invested with nearly limitless authority, provided they were "cool" of course.

The Oaf escaped some of his oafishness by a discreet choosing of the authorities who would let him excel. He became an acceptable country singer and found himself, somewhat to his surprise, the leader of a country-and-western band composed entirely of relations and what our clan called "near relations."

Who gave weight to those authorities? No one is more conventional than a teen-aged boy, and the Oaf was no exception to this rule. Basically, his conventions gave him a choice of personal dictators. Perhaps the range, the sheer size of his family and the diversity of his unquestionable church was his salvation, as well as his group of musician friends who afforded him a very effective protective coloration while he searched for what he was capable of and what he would do with it. Being cast in the role of The Oaf wasn't all bad. It afforded him the position jesters have always enjoyed, a role apart, a position from which to observe.

It is clear enough by now that if our clown had to choose between dictators, he was capable of making do with the conventions offered him. He manipulated his own family symbols with great dexterity. His emergence from high school offered him a new choice of conventions. In one ingenious wriggle he escaped the position of clown in his family by doing a very respectable thing; he became a Benedictine monk a full thousand miles from his family home. An older brother in the monastery lent further respectability. His musical talent was to develop and his college education to begin under the aegis of the Abbey of Our Lady of Perpetual Help.

A small world, you say, and indeed it was. Family and friends were Roman Catholic all, as was his schooling, his ambition and his hopes. Within this group, however, he learned the harsh skills of dealing with ridicule and failure. If at this stage he had little chance to practice taking the role of others, being the low man on the totem pole, his later career as an exceptionally talented and humorous therapist bears out his profit from his days of being The Oaf. When his stage was larger, a well of hard-earned compassion appeared that brought him a national reputation as a therapist, mixed as it was not only with love but with dexterously aimed barbs of humorous provocation. I cannot but remember that his music in his high school days was "country," the constant themes of

185

which are destruction and betrayal. Even then he was reaching out to pain and confusion. That reaching came to form later in a truly ingenious way.

What were the sources and challenges to his faith? The word "congruence" comes to mind—that was his challenge. He needed to find a world that would take him seriously in the relatively narrow paths available to him. The artfulness of his tight-rope-walking in a family where he was daily threatened with oblivion stood him in good stead. If his immediate family were parochial folk, they were also proud and uncommonly intelligent, most of them. If his family were prone to ridicule him, as a group they stuck together like glue against all other comers. If both his sense of faith and his Identity were derived at this point in his life, they were **artfully** derived and left the door open for more artful and more autonomous faith and Identity later on.

We leave him at the gates of the monastery in Portsmouth, New Hampshire. He is dressed severely in black—black Stetson on his head, a gift from an older brother, and black Brooks Brothers' suit on his back, thanks to the generosity of his well-to-do aunt. The cowboy/monk solution is not final. It is one of many rebirths still in process.

4. Caroline at Thirty

"Individuating-reflexive" faith. This faith/knowing is aware of polarities in human living such as self-fulfillment vs. service to others, individuality vs. community, relative vs. absolute truth. It begins the task of taking responsibility for the commitments made in a relativistic world. It tends toward an ideological perspective and is often deeply affected by charismatic leaders.

A woman in her physical prime, living with her husband and two small children in an apartment on Paris' Left Bank, was one of that same family, like the others; but she had made her jump, as her cousin The Oaf had not. Her way of knowing **authority** was more individuated than his. Her notion of ultimate authority lay in the group she had chosen. She paid great attention to the American community of artists, writers and painters in the Paris of the nineteen-sixties. She labelled herself a writer and strove mightily to be whatever a writer was.

Her own affinities were important to her. Paris seemed a place "sympatique." She wanted to live her way, simply, almost starkly. She spoke to me of wanting to wander alone on foot through the small roads of the south of France for a whole summer. I remember how intensely she said she wanted to do that. Her authorities were her affinities and her now chosen ideologies as writer, marriage partner and intellectual, separate now from the all-inclusive Catholocism we knew as children.

She weighed those new authorities endlessly, self-consciously, and fiercely. Did her writing really fit? Did her husband and children fit her? There was a dimension of rootlessness—the struggle to leave behind a strong church. A primal struggle that she seemed unable to wholly pull off. She had a beachhead of her own in Paris, in her career, her own children and marriage partner, her "circle"...but there was trouble holding it.

God knows, she was intelligent. She saw the holes in her religious tradition and her family's insularity, its hidebound approach to Midwestern American gentility.

I think of a room in her apartment in Paris which, whenever I visited it, had a large geometric arrangement of small stones neatly laid out on the wooden floor. Each time I came, every month or so, I found the design changed but always the arrangement—fanlike, precise, like a large shell laid out in tiny pieces on the floor.

I think of her paintings, done on varnished wood—strange bird-like animals in one-line drawings—always neat, always eccentric, always possessed of giant eyes. Peacocks with ostrich legs and fishlike eyes, in peacock colors. Flat, oval owls in white, quiet and looking, always looking.

It was as if she had left one rich and exacting system of family, career and religion and was trying to reproduce another of her own, her very own, with all the exactitude, precision and law she had left behind.

187

Her concern was with getting things just so. She didn't mail her poems or her novels to any publisher. They were kept, like her stones on the floor, safe for her own revision and apart from the comments of editors across the sea.

It was this concern for aptness that led to solitude. We talked once about her walking the streets with her small shopping net for groceries, thinking she could not bring herself to talk to the baker, or the butcher, or the fish monger. This was not out of snobbery, but for fear she would not say it right, though her French was nearly faultless.

To identify with and take the part of a group was difficult. Her standards were high, her designs shifting. She seemed drifting in alternate stages of despair and anger, to take the part of groups that were imaginary, farther and father from flesh and blood.

Her faith was challenged by the reality of human groups. It was a challenge of trust, the call to risk some sort of human unit outside herself. She was taxed to test the boundaries of convention. Facing the boundaries of a middle-class Catholic background was a wrench that caused her to leave it. To find once more the boundaries of new conventions and to transcend them was a challenge. American Paris intellectuals can be as boring as Midwestern suburbanites. She told me that once. I think the challenge was to "make do" with the limitations of her own self-chosen world. It is the challenge of sometimes rueful laughter.

Instead of laughter I found in her a sort of fierce attempt to walk on the water lying between the land of home and roots to the small boat she had chosen for her own. Her face was a brave front, young but gaunt and drawn, her eyes flashing, her lips purposefully and carefully pronouncing approval or disapproval, but seldom the abandon of joy. The challenge of a channelled way of knowing the forces of the world seemed at this point to be not only beyond her hold, but well beyond her reach. An enduring trust was not there.

5. Himself at Fifty

"Paradoxical-consolidative" faith. A way of knowing that is

fully aware of the price of making one commitment instead of another. This point of view recognizes truth in other positions than its own. It regards as brother and sister those beyond one's own tribe, race, and creed. It has regard for those even in opposition to it. This wide identification with others is accompanied by the agony of loyalty to one's still-held more narrow affiliations. There is a sense of tension here.

At fifty his authorities, the biggest ones, were dead, separated, or assimilated. The contributors? He had spent nearly half his life as a member of a Catholic religious order— the Jesuits. In the ten years since the ordeal of leaving them, he had gotten a Ph.D. in Canada, had married a woman of intellect and courage, and obtained a teaching position at a large Midwestern university in the social sciences. The priestly caste, the way of obedience, and a lifelong celibacy had all given way to other ways of living less brahminesque.

His authorities had been his family, his Church, and his superiors as a priest. In gradually loosening the external grip of these strong folk, his authority had come more to center in himself.

The father of Joseph and Matthew, cousin of The Oaf, and brother of Caroline had had a time of it personalizing his approach to his very Catholic gods and demons. He had known down deep that the mark of his church and priesthood were too much a part of him to wipe away. Once he was relegated to second-class citizenship in the process his church uses in allowing priests to marry, he had been only dimly aware how much of his life's work would have to be refitted and changed. The man who had learned to live quite nicely and adroitly within the caste of the priesthood got a positive case of the bends in taking himself seriously as a good, creative, and priestly person with nobody around to tell him what to do or approve "officially" of his own necessary resynthesis of belief and occupation. He began to see rather slowly as a social scientist with a theological background that there might be work of dignity in bringing his science to bear on the broadly religious concerns of himself and his students.

The wider community in which he began to live in his

189

forties piqued his curiosity and opened very slowly a hope of touching the minds and hearts of his students with a message not precisely religious but one which could help them assess their religious backgrounds and critically to examine them. He felt a sense of exhilaration when he noted that the world of academe was very thin when it came to speaking intellectually to the religious backgrounds of undergraduates in state schools. It came upon him one day that he had absolutely no desire that his students become Catholic, Christian or formally religiously affiliated at all. Then he had to pinch himself to see if he himself had thought like that, "and him a Catholic priest!"

"Oh yes," his inner voice replied. "You are still one of them. For God's sake don't be silly and pretend you're not—or worse, wait for the day when your own people accept your work. That would be ridiculous."

That inner voice was his own voice, but he found it hard to accept. He felt deeply the pull between his Catholic self and the wider community around it. He knew that he had sawed off blithely the limb of his outer voices and that he had damned well better listen to the inner ones.

His thinking was a long time coming to see that the language of the human mind admits of necessity many different answers to any really important question. He began to see the question of commitment as the question of faith. What a relief for him to see that he could commit himself to his God as a Catholic and be helpful at the same time to others making their own style of commitment.

His own list of great human beings included an awful swatch of religious styles. Gandhi, Martin Luther, Lincoln, Albert Schweitzer, and Malcolm X need not be measured against Jesus and the God of Israel, but alongside them and in the midst of them.

His great symbolic tradition began to come back to him— the creeds he had cared for and carped over, the crucifix he had loved and then dreaded, the feast of the Resurrection which had caused him such joy and such doubt, all these and more were coming slowly back to him in a new and more

190

touching form. There was something behind all those symbols that became richer as he let them touch him once more— richer than any ideological explanation of exactly what they meant or signified.

And his ability to identify with his fellow humans? Slowly it became wider. He liked to think that there were no longer any outsiders.

"I would welcome the diversity of humankind; each person is my sister or my brother. I need not baptize any but my own, nor are my own any better than those who are not," he wrote in his journal.

There is an anguish in new-found, or almost found, universalism. He knew now he had cut himself off from the majority of his own church, including many of its "official" teachings. He knew that half his family regarded him as a rather harmless religious fanatic, the other half as a traitor. He longed for the comfort of his father's house, as the Prodigal Son did in Luke's gospel. He longed still for the unalloyed joy of presiding at worship in his church and the aura of the caste of priesthood. He still caught himself hoping to wake up tomorrow to get on with business the way it used to be, as perhaps many have hoped when the dust has settled around a deeply religious time of growth. Oh for the old days!

And the source of his faith? Its source was the strength of the man who has found he has a good way of knowing and feeling his deepest values. Perhaps not the best way, certainly not the only way. But good? Rich? Old? Alive? Yes.

His faith was challenged by its loneliness. Not many of his family or his old priest friends had come to this paradoxical form of believing. He knew as well that the rifts between himself and his church would never close. Among his secular friends he knew he would always be an eccentric. For the first time in his life he knew he had many wounds in himself that would never heal, and many differences between himself and his colleagues and friends which would never be reconciled.

He was presented with a grave challenge to be ethically responsible, and this in a world he knew well enough to be ambiguous. Ambiguity or no, it was a challenge to his

191

faith/knowing that he stand and be counted when he knew he had often been not only wrong in his past stands, but arrogant as well. His challenge was the challenge of making peace in a world that did not know peace. To tell the truth with a mind that knew there are many truths. To be assuring without laying aside his own doubts. In his own tradition, it was the challenge that dared hope for resurrection while not denying the grisly sight of the Man naked on the cross.

6. Ann at Seventy-five

"Universalizing" faith. If the preceding stage is characterized by a broad community, it is also a stage of struggle and agony over past but still-felt narrower loyalties. This stage passes beyond the struggle. There is a sense of simplicity and unity. There is a kinship for other faiths, an undiluted sense of brother and sisterhood that cuts across all denominational and theist lines.

I shall here warn the reader that in my opinion Ann does not really represent Fowler's stage six. She has been an ideologue (stage 4) in her mature years and those of her old age as well. Something remarkably like Fowler's last stage came about in her during the last two months of her life. She is as close to Fowler's last stage as the author could find in his own extended family. I don't think she ever formally and deliberately removed herself from her ideological approach to faith/knowing. She was, however, certainly allowing her left hand to move in this direction, while not acknowledging this movement with her right.

An old lady is dying of cancer of the colon. She knows it. The last month or two of her life are in process. She is the grandmother of Joe and Matthew, aunt of The Oaf, the mother of Caroline and her brother, whom I call "himself."

She has been the matriarch of an extended family, a woman of great power in her blood circle. Her finger has been in the lives of us all. Her hand with us has represented strict religion and a strong, almost overpowering sense of duty. Her reign has been long, like Victoria's.

Now, at the end, who told her what to do? No one, it seemed. I found it remarkable that the rituals preceding death seemed of little importance to her, and that she talked very little of religion. There was a reality that made religious talk seem like small talk. She knew this was the event of her life.

Her absorption with preserving her dignity and facing her own end was not an obsession, just a reality. She was concerned really with only one person...her one living daughter (not Caroline—Caroline O'Connell ended her own life by suicide at the age of thirty-six), in whose life she had gently and brutally meddled for fifty years. She wanted to give back something. She wanted to hand on something. The two women spent long hours together day after day those last two months. Near the end she gave her daughter her own wedding rings, not to keep, but to wear. I cannot ask anyone really to grasp the heavy equality of tha gesture who did not know the years of struggle that preceded it.

With the rest of us she had time to be urbane, it is true, but there was the one great peace to be made and she knew it. They both knew it. It was a matter of discipline and opportunity. There was only strength and opportunity for one big effort other than dying itself. She husbanded her forces for it.

Her life had never been simple before, always the Old Curiosity Shop of a house, importunations, bills, donations, meticulous charities. That was gone now. To her daughter she said, disarmingly, "You know dear, I have never done this before."

The old religious battles were gone. She had been a great measurer of orthodoxy and morality in her time. She knew the real Catholics from those who didn't measure up, whether morally or according to rightness of belief.

I sat in that bare hospital room where she died when a young priest confidant of hers came to pay his last wishes and to introduce her to his wife. Heretofore she had said some rather strong things about Catholic priests deserting their ministry for marriage. This was over now. She was very tired.

On his entrance with his wife she quietly rallied, assured him that she was ready to die in a firm, quiet voice and then cast her famous appraising look on his wife. She had wilted many a strong flower with that queenly look over the years. It searched for orthodoxy, courage, and good manners. As her old eyes were levelly greeted with the grey eyes of her priest's wife, she looked only for courage and gentility. Religious correctness was not an issue. And so, quickly, before she would lose her strength, the quiet words of approval, encouragement and hope—an assurance of a good future. There was no struggle or sense of paradox. I stood in the door and thought through my own tears, "I've never seen her like this before. It's simpler. She's as judgmental as ever, but now it's simpler, no side issues, no law but her own."

Her thinking? How to put it? It had a directness and a focus—always the same context—the cliff's edge. Nothing could get between her and it. When she came into the hospital from home for the last time, after collapsing there, my brother-in-law and I drove out to see her, thinking it was over. She was cheerful and revived and in need of her bedpan when we arrived. She dismissed us after a minute or two. "Run along now, boys," she said. It was as though she had important work to do. She let us go almost gaily to get on with it.

I have mentioned that she didn't spend a lot of time on the rest of us, although she did like our presence. One of us was there quietly twenty-four hours a day for the last two weeks. She had no accounts to settle except one. It was a withdrawal that did not strike me as difficult for her. It was a gradual absorption with something else, firm, quiet, and of course, polite.

What carried her through and what were her challenges at the end?

I know there was the challenge of despair. Her work was not finished. She cried a little once in front of me and said in her tears, "I feel like I'm running out on Bob." Bob was her husband. In giving her rings to her daughter she was accepting inevitable tragedies, passing them on. She and her

194

daughter had a delightful conversation about how important it was to be "top dog." She gave that away too. Down deep she thought that really **nobody** could replace her, and of course, nobody could. That was a challenge to her faith.

It is traditional in my family to exaggerate the faults and virtues of one another in life, thus giving us an excuse to brag and be meddlesome. In death we generally so distort those who have gone as to rob them of any credibility whatsoever. I don't think the thought of that eventuality bothered Ann. Her ending days were too busy. She managed quite nicely to screen out of her last months anybody likely to be fawning or obsequious. They just didn't get in to see her.

Her focus **was** from time to time interrupted by those of us with vested interests. Indeed there were some rather dramatic plays for a larger share of her attention, but she saved most of it for one person. The surgeon who pulled for chemotherapy didn't get much house. The four or five different priests who each separately felt called upon to give her the last rites of the church were peripheral. There was an officious nun or two. "Himself's" bewilderment and her husband's state of shock were challenges, but she chose to keep them away from the center.

The challenges to the faith of this old lady were reduced to two—to trust her daughter and the rest of the world she symbolized to carry on without her, and to suffer the indignity and embarrassment to which her own failing body brutally subjected her. Throwing up is not dignified, nor is being unable to tend to your hair. Ann had a hard time imagining any benign Ultimate Power who would allow her to vomit in the presence of others or to appear dishevelled. I rather think she did not forgive her God for these last two visitations. Nor is she likely to. It is hard for me to imagine as well that in another life she could pass up the chance, if given, to get in a little skillful meddling in the lives of those who might need it, as well as those who might not.

C. Coda: Ann's funeral

Ann saved her last hurrah for after death. She and her

195

daughter worked out every detail of her funeral. Twelve pall bearers were summoned from both coasts and parts in between. Her nephew Thomas, elder brother of John, was to say the Mass and preach. John, who had once been The Oaf, was to sing. The three eldest male grandchildren were to read the scriptures. "Himself" was to work out the coordinating and summoning of the principals. She wanted the cheapest coffin that could be bought, covered in its entirety with a blanket of daisies for the wake. A second blanket of daisies for the funeral itself, no wilted flowers for her on *her* exit.

All those who were summoned came. John (according to instructions) sang a mixture of Protestant hymns, *Onward Christian Soldiers,* and Roman chant, *In Paradisum.* Through my own tears I saw at that ceremony a single community singing and marching to Communion. Intercommunion is **not** a Roman Catholic tradition. I counted among those taking an active part atheists, agnostics, Baptists, proper Episcopalians and unchurched folk. The pall bearers were not all men of virtue (they **were** all men, I must admit), nor were they all religious in any formal sense. They were **her** young men, whether they had "turned out" well or not.

Her widest community and her widest range of acceptance came to life in that ritual. And of course we all knew that she had planned it. She had planned or at least dabbled in the lives of every person in that huge Byzantine cathedral. With the exception of Caroline, each of the subjects of these sketches was there. Matthew facing his first real desertion, inexplicable but at least acknowledged and certainly interesting. He tried to look under the cover of the grave at the cemetery to see if there really was a hole there. Joe, investing still in his "good guys"—and they were nearly all there, with the possible exception of John Travolta and Johnny Bench. John, so long ago The Oaf, singing her choices, but very much his way. And Caroline? It is in my tradition that she could have a place, with the pictures and mosaics of people gone but remembered, the statues, the tombs of former bishops. The fanlike patterns of the mosaics in that great church now remind me of her patterned stones on the floor of that Paris apartment. The one I have called "Himself" was there too, of course, hear to splitting amid his paradoxes, very fragile that day, but not likely to forget it as a challenge to his new-found wider community. Perhaps this was his mother Ann's gift to him, to see and experience in his own church that which before he had only understood when he felt most outside her.

One family then, six very different people, drawn together by the death of one of them. Each one seen in this essay at a special time of faith, a time which will underlay future passages of faithing just as surely as it relies upon its past ones. We leave you now, and hope you will remember us.

197

EPILOGUE

This book has been a series of reflections on the teaching of human development. Its tone and content swing chapter by chapter, from Apollo to Dionysius, from abstraction to concrete example, from rationalism to poetry. It is dedicated to the proposition that in each student and teacher there lurks both poet and rationalist. As in the course of human development there are patterns in which either the rationalist or the poet in each of us is likely to be prominent.

It is further dedicated to the proposition that each teacher must discover the peculiar genius of her own stage of development and put this talent to work in a way most apt to touch the patterns of strength fitting the stages of the students around her. What Erik Erikson once said of the effective therapist goes as well for the effective teacher—"My task is to help you weather your crisis in a way consonant with the way I weather my own."

Francis L. Gross, Jr.

WRITINGS ON WHICH THIS BOOK IS BASED

CHAPTER I. "The University as Asylum," in *Perspectives*, Vol. 7, No. 1, Spring, 1975.

CHAPTER II. "Using Small Groups in Undergraduate Teaching," *Perspectives*, Vol. 6, No. 2, Fall, 1974

CHAPTER III. "Ethical Issues in Undergraduate Teaching," *The University College Quarterly*, Vol. 24, No. 1, November, 1978.

CHAPTER IV. "Week by Week, Hour by Hour (A Teacher's Journal of a General Studies Course)," *Perspectives*, Vol. 8, No. 1, Fall, 1976.

CHAPTER V. "Erikson and Perry on Intellectual Development," *Free Inquiry in Creative Sociology*, Vol. 9, No. 1, May, 1981.

CHAPTER VI. "Kohlberg vs. Perry: Moral Development Theory," *Free Inquiry in Creative Sociology*, Vol. 8, No. 2, November, 1980.

CHAPTER VII. "Reflections on Cognitive-Moral Development in a Jesuit Education," *The Journal of General Education*, Vol. 32, No. 1, Spring, 1980.

CHAPTER VIII. "Teaching Cognitive-Moral Development in College (A Generalist Approach)," *The Journal of General Education*, Vol. 32, No. 4, Winter, 1981.

CHAPTER IX. "Teaching the Whole Mind: A Developmental-Structuralist Approach," an address given at The Adult Development Conference, Georgia State University, Atlanta, Georgia, September, 1980.

CHAPTER X. "A Sequential Sextet (Portraits of Faith Stages in One Family)," *The Journal of General Education*, Vol. 32, No. 2, Summer, 1981.

FOOTNOTES*

CHAPTER I. THE UNIVERSITY AS ASYLUM

1. *The Holy Bible*, Revised Standard Version. Camden: Thomas Nelson, 1952. Genesis, Ch. 6, vv. 1-9.
2. Carol Travis, "What Does College Do For a Person? Frankly Very Little," in *Psychology Today*, September, 1974, p. 73.
3. "Too Many A's," in *Time*, November 11, 1974, p. 106.
4. Erik H. Erikson, *Young Man Luther*. New York: Norton, 1958, 1962, p. 14.
5. Erik H. Erikson, *Youth: Identity and Crisis*. New York: 1968, p. 28.
6. James Brodrick, *St. Ignatius Loyola, The Pilgrim Years*. London: Burns and Dates, 1956, vii-372.
7. *Ibid.*, p. 82.
8. *Ibid.*, p. 152.
9. *Ibid.*, p. 152.
10. *Ibid.*, p. 278.
11. Ignatius Loyola, *The Spiritual Exercises of Saint Ignatius*, translated by Anthony Motta. Garden City: Image Books, 1964, p. 1-200.
12. *Young Man Luther*, pp. 1-288.
13. *Ibid.*, p. 53.
14. *Ibid.*, p. 90.
15. *Ibid.*, p. 98.
16. *Ibid.*, p. 66.
17. *Ibid.*, p. 251.
18. Erik H. Erikson, *Gandhi's Truth*. New York: Norton, 1968, p. 139 ff, p. 170.
19. *Ibid.*, pp. 143, 145, 147.
20. *Ibid.*, pp. 168 ff.
21. *Ibid.*, p. 142.
22. *Ibid.*, p. 143, (underline mine).
23. Malcom X, *The Autobiography of Malcolm X*. New York: Grove Press, 1964, pp. 9-10.
24. *Ibid.*, pp. 25-31.

*Note should be made of these publications which have appeared since the completion of this book. They are recent important statements by authors who have been referred to repeatedly in this book.

The Philosophy of Moral Development, by Lawrence Kohlberg. New York: Harper and Row, 1981.

Stages of Faith, by James W. Fowler. New York: Harper and Row, 1981.

25. *Ibid.*, pp. 39-150.
26. *Ibid.*, p. 151.
27. *Ibid.*, p. 161 ff.
28. *Ibid.*, p. 172.
29. *Ibid.*, p. 173.
30. *Ibid.*, p. 179.
31. *Youth: Identity and Crisis*, pp. 156-157.
32. *Ibid.*, pp. 96-107.
33. *The Holy Bible*, Luke, Ch. 17, vv. 3-4, Matthew Ch. 18, vv. 21-23.
34. *Youth: Identity and Crisis*, p. 182.
35. *Ibid.*, pp. 107-114.
36. *Ibid.*, pp. 183-184.
37. *Ibid.*, pp. 115-122.
38. *Ibid.*, p. 184
39. *Ibid.*, pp. 122-128.
40. *Ibid.*, p. 185.
41. *Ibid.*, pp. 93-96, 180.
42. *Ibid.*, pp. 135-138.
43. *Ibid.*, pp. 185-187.
44. *Ibid.*, pp. 137-139.
45. *Ibid.*, p. 187.
46. *Young Man Luther*, p. 66.
47. *Youth: Identity and Crisis*, pp. 139-141.
48. *Ibid.*, pp. 187-188 (underline mine).
49. *The Autobiography of Malcom X*, pp. 323-342.
50. *Ibid.*, pp. 288-317.
51. *Gandhi's Truth*, pp. 395-409, esp. p. 397.
52. *The Spiritual Exercises of Saint Ignatius*, pp. 139-142.
53. *Ibid.*, pp. 129-134.
54. *Young Man Luther*, pp. 76, 178-195.
55. *Ibid.*, p. 122.

CHAPTER II. USING SMALL GROUPS IN UNDERGRADUATE TEACHING

1. Herbert C. Kelman, "Processes of Opinion Change," in *Planning of Change*, edited by Warren G. Bennis, Kenneth D. Denne, and Robert Chin. New York: Holt, Rinehart and Winston, 1961, pp. 509-517.
2. Thomas Aquinas, *Truth*, translated by James V. McGlynn. Chicago: Regnery, 1953, vol. II, pp. 81, 83.
3. Jack Horn, "Clues for Tired Teaching," in *Psychology Today*, July, 1974, pp. 25-26.
4. Marvin E. Shaw, *Group Dynamics: The Psychology of the Small Group*. New York: McGraw-Hill, 1971, pp. 67-68.
5. *Ibid.*, p. 396.
6. *Ibid.*, pp. 118-122, 149.

7. *Ibid.*, pp. 137-148, 151-152.
8. *Ibid.*, pp. 166-167, 183.
9. *Ibid.*, pp. 168-169, 183-184.
10. *Ibid.*, p. 147.
11. J. William Pfeiffer and John E. Jones, *A Handbook of Structured Experiences for Human Relations Training.* Iowa City: University Associates Press, 1969, vol. 1, pp. 19-20, vol. III. pp. 3-5.
12. Shaw, pp. 192-205, 228-230.
13. *Ibid.*, pp. 216-228, 230-231.
14. *Ibid.*, pp. 241-244, 281.
15. *Ibid.*, pp. 258-259, 284-285.
16. *Ibid.*, pp. 274-279, 286-287.
17. *Ibid.*, pp. 289-290, 326.
18. *Ibid.*, pp. 321, 330-331.
19. Erik Erikson, *Youth: Identity and Crisis.* Norton: 1968, pp. 1-336.
20. J. D. Salinger, *The Catcher in the Rye.* New York: Bantam, 1951, pp. 1-214.
21. Shaw, pp. 294-300, 326.
22. *Ibid.*, pp. 318-319, 329.
23. *Ibid.*, pp. 318, 329.
24. *Ibid.*, pp. 73-79, 82-83.
25. *Ibid.*, pp. 315-316, 328.
26. *Ibid.*, pp. 320, 330.
27. *Ibid.*, p. 81.
28. *Ibid.*, p. 82.

CHAPTER III. ETHICAL ISSUES: AN ERIKSONIAN PERSPECTIVE

1. Erik H. Erikson, *Identity: Youth and Crisis.* New York: Norton, 1968, pp. 91-141.
2. Erik H. Erikson, *Insight and Responsibility.* New York: Norton, 1964, pp. 219-243.
3. *Ibid.*, p. 220 (underline mine).
4. *Ibid.*, p. 233.
5. Erik H. Erikson, *Life History and the Historical Moment.* New York: Norton, 1975, . 218-219.
6. Erik H. Erikson, *Dimensions of a New Identity.* New York: Norton, 1974, p. 14.
7. Erik H. Erikson, *Life History and the Historical Moment.* p. 116.
8. *Ibid.*, p. 116.
9. *Ibid.*, p. 236.
10. Erik H. Erikson, *Insight and Responsibility*, p. 173-174.
11. Erik H. Erikson, *Childhood and Society.* New York: Norton, 1950, 1963, pp. 247-274. *Insight and Responsibility*, pp. 100-107, pp. 111-134. *Identity: Youth and Crisis*, pp. 91-141.
12. Susan Friedman, editor, *Annual Editions: Readings in Human*

Development 75/76. Guilford Dushkin Publishing Group, 1975, pp. 21-34.
13. Erik H. Erikson, *Identity: Youth and Crisis*, pp. 216-221.
14. *Ibid.*, pp. 179-188.
15. *Ibid.*, p. 28.
16. Erik H. Erikson, *Young Man Luther*. New York: Norton, 1958, p. 14.
17. Erik H. Erikson, *Insight and Responsibility*, p. 220.
18. Erik H. Erikson, *Identity: Youth and Crisis*, pp. 181-182.
19. *Ibid.*, p. 96-107.
20. Erik H. Erikson, *Childhood and Society*, pp. 266-267.
21. Erik H. Erikson, *Dimensions of a New Identity*, p. 124.
22. Erik H. Erikson, *Insight and Responsibility*, p. 231.
23. Erik H. Erikson, *Life History and the Historical Moment*, p. 218.
24. Erik H. Erikson, *Dimensions of a New Identity*, p. 49.
25. Erik H. Erikson, *Identity: Youth and Crisis*, p. 183.
26. *Ibid.*, pp. 107-114; *Childhood and Society*, pp. 251-254.
27. Erik H. Erikson, *Insight and Responsibility*, p. 97.
28. Erik H. Erikson, *Identity: Youth and Crisis*, p. 184.
29. *Ibid.*, pp. 115-122, *Childhood and Society*, pp. 255-258.
30. Erik H. Erikson, *Dimensions of a New Identity*, p. 104.
31. Erik H. Erikson, *Life History and the Historical Moment*, pp. 128-235.
32. *Ibid.*, pp. 171-172.
33. *Ibid.*, p. 205; *Dimensions of a New Identity*, p. 107.
34. Erik H. Erikson, *Identity: Youth and Crisis*, pp. 184-185.
35. *Ibid.*, pp. 135-138; *Childhood and Society*, pp. 258-261.
36. Erik H. Erikson, *Insight and Responsibility*, p. 98.
37. Erik H. Erikson, *Life History and the Historical Moment*, p. 187.
38. Erik H. Erikson, *Identity: Youth and Crisis*, p. 186.
39. *Ibid.*, pp. 135-138; *Childhood and Society*, pp. 263-266.
40. Erik H. Erikson, *Life History and the Historical Moment*, p. 254.
41. Erik H. Erikson, *Identity: Youth and Crisis*, p. 187.
42. *Ibid.*, pp. 138-139; *Childhood and Society*, pp. 266-268.
43. Erik H. Erikson, *Dimensions of a New Identity*, p. 102.
44. Erik H. Erikson, *Identity: Youth and Crisis*, pp. 187-188; *Life History and the Historical Moment*, pp. 206-207.
45. Erik H. Erikson, *Identity: Youth and Crisis*, pp. 139-141; *Childhood and Society*, pp. 268-269.
46. Erik H. Erikson, *Life History and the Historical Moment*, pp. 206-207.
47. *Ibid.*, p. 204.
48. Erik H. Erikson, *Gandhi's Truth*. New York: Norton, 1969, pp. 396-397.
49. Erik H. Erikson, *Dimensions of a New Identity*, p. 108.

CHAPTER IV. A TEACHER'S JOURNAL

1. I refer the reader to Chapter Two of this book.
2. *Idem*.

CHAPTER V. INTELLECTUAL DEVELOPMENT IN THE UNDERGRADUATE: ERIKSON AND PERRY

1. William G. Perry, Jr., *Forms of Intellectual and Ethical Development in the College Years, a Scheme*. New York: Holt, Rinehart and Winston, 1968, 1970, v-256.
2. Erik H. Erikson, *Identity, Youth and Crisis*. New York: Norton, 1968, 336 pp. *Young Man Luther*. New York: Norton, 1958, 288 pp. All of Erikson's books deal in some way with the issue of identity. I take these two to be central.
3. *Young Man Luther*, p. 134.
4. *Ibid.*, pp. 118, 134.
5. *Ibid.*, p. 157.
6. *Identity, Youth and Crisis*, pp. 233-236.
7. Forms of Intellectual and Ethical Development in the College Years, "Chart of Development."
8. *Ibid.*, p. 97. Perry's work begins with interviews in the Spring of the student's freshman year. He infers dualistic thought on the part of most entering freshmen, pp. 59-88.
9. *Forms of Intellectual and Ethical Development in the College Years*, "Chart of Development," pp. 153-155.
10. *Ibid.*, "Glossary."
11. *Ibid.*, "Glossary."
12. *Identity, Youth and Crisis*, p. 19.
13. *Identity, Youth and Crisis, pp. 156-157; Young Man Luther*, p. 133.
14. *Forms of Intellectual and Ethical Development*, pp. 178-182.
15. Lewis C. Soloman, "Too Many College Graduates"? in *Relating Work and Education*, edited by Dyckman W. Vermilye. San Francisco: Jossey-Bass, 1977, p. 172-181.
16. *Forms of Intellectual and Ethical Development*, pp. 182-189.
17. *Forms of Intellectual and Ethical Development*, pp. 190-198.
18. *Young Man Luther*, pp. 105-110; *Identity, Youth and Crisis*, pp. 172-176.
19. *Forms of Intellectual and Ethical Development*, pp. 72-73.
20. *Young Man Luther*, pp. 118, 134-135, 150.
21. *Identity, Youth and Crisis*, p. 314.
22. Erik H. Erikson, *Insight and Responsibility*. New York: Norton, 1964, pp. 170, 173-175.
23. *Young Man Luther*, pp. 103-104.
24. *Young Man Luther*, pp. 103-104.
25. *Forms of Intellectual and Ethical Development*, pp. 121-122.
26. *Young Man Luther*, pp. 166-169.

27. *Forms of Intellectual and Ethical Development*, pp. 213-215.
28. *Ibid.*, pp. 72-73.
29. *Ibid.*, pp. 109-116.
30. *Ibid.*, p. 122.
31. *Insight and Responsibility*, p. 174.
32. Gail Sheehy, *Passages (Predictable Crisis of Adult Life)*. New York: Bantam, 1974, pp. 189-190.

CHAPTER VI. KOHLBERG VERSUS PERRY ON MORAL DEVELOPMENT

1. William G. Perry, Jr., *Forms of Intellectual and Ethical Development in the College Years: A Scheme* (New York, 1970), p. 9.
2. Lawrence Kohlberg, *The Development of Modes of Moral Thinking and Choice in the Years Ten to Sixteen* (Chicago, 1958). Unpublished doctoral dissertation.
3. Lawrence Kohlberg, "From Is to Ought," *Cognitive Development and Epistemology*, Theodore Mischel, ed. (New York, 1971), pp. 163-174.
4. *Ibid.*, p. 164 (emphasis mine).
5. *Ibid.*, p. 164.
6. Perry, *op. cit.*, pp. 69, 71, 84.
7. *Ibid.*, pp. 67, 85.
8. *Ibid.*, pp. 84-88.
9. *Ibid.*, p. 76.
10. *Ibid.*, p. 85.
11. *Ibid.*, p. 90.
12. *Ibid.*, Glossary (emphasis mine).
13. Lawrence Kohlberg and Carol Gilligan, "The Adolescent as Philosopher," *Daedalus* (Fall, 1971), p. 1061.
14. Kohlberg, "From Is to Ought," pp. 193-195.
15. Perry, *op cit.*, p. 109.
16. Kohlberg and Gilligan, "The Adolescent as Philosopher," p. 1061.
17. Perry, *op. cit.*, pp. 116-122.
18. Kohlberg and Gilligan, "The Adolescent as Philosopher," p. 1075.
19. *Ibid.*, p. 1077.
20. *Ibid.*, p. 1078.
21. Erik H. Erikson, *Childhood and Society* (2nd ed., New York, 1963), p. 262. See also my essay contrasting the work of Erikson and Perry, *Intellectual Development in the Undergraduate* (Kalamazoo, 1978). Unpublished essay.
22. Perry, *op. cit.*, pp. 122-126.
23. Kohlberg and Gilligan, "The Adolescent as Philosopher," p. 1081.
24. Perry, *op. cit.*, pp. 126-128.
25. *Ibid.*, pp. 177-200.
26. Kohlberg and Gilligan, "The Adolescent as Philosopher," p. 1075.
27. *Ibid.*, pp. 174, 1080.

28. Perry, *op. cit.*, pp. 128-133.
29. Kohlberg and Gilligan, "The Adolescent as Philosopher," p. 1078. Kohlberg, "From Is to Ought," pp. 203-204.
30. Perry, *op. cit.*, p. 153.
31. Kohlberg, "From Is to Ought," p. 164 (emphasis mine).
32. Kohlberg, "Moral Development in Aging Human Beings," *The Gerontologist*, Vol. 13, No. 4 (1973), p. 500.
33. Perry, *op. cit.*, p. 14.
34. *Ibid.*, p. 135.
35. Erik H. Erikson, *Young Man Luther* (New York, 1958), p. 14.
36. Perry, *op. cit.*, p. 14.
37. Kohlberg, "From Is to Ought," pp. 151-155.
38. *Ibid.*, p. 165.
39. Perry, *op. cit.*, pp. 135-136.
40. *Ibid.*, p. 155.
41. Kohlberg, "From Is to Ought," pp. 201-203.
42. *Ibid.*, pp. 190-193.

CHAPTER VII. REFLECTIONS ON COGNITIVE-MORAL DEVELOPMENT IN A JESUIT EDUCATION

1. The author was a member of the Missouri Province of the Society of Jesus from 1949-1969. He studied at St. Louis University, the Institute of Pastoral and Cathechetical Studies in Brussels, and Fordham University. After leaving the Jesuits he received his Ph.D. from the University of Ottawa. He is presently Associate Professor of Social Science at Western Michigan University.
2. Lawrence Kohlberg is the director of The Center for Moral Education, Graduate School of Education, Harvard University.
3. L. Kohlberg, "The Cognitive-Developmental Approach to Education," in *The Phi Delta Kappan*, June 1975, p. 672.
4. L. Kohlberg and C. Gilligan, "The Adolescent as Philosopher: The Discovery of Self in a Postconventional World," *Daedalus*, 100, No. 4, Fall, 1972, pp. 1066-1071.
5. Kohlberg, "The Cognitive-Developmental Approach to Education," p. 671.
6. L. Kohlberg, "The Child as a Moral Philosopher," *Psychology Today*, 7 (1968) pp. 26-30.
7. L. Kohlberg, P. Scharf, and J. Hickey, "The Justice Structure of the Prison: A Theory and an Intervention," *The Prison Journal*, Autumn-Winter, 1972.
8. Kohlberg and Gilligan, "Adolescent as Philosopher," p. 1067.
9. *Ibid.*, p. 1067.
10. *Ibid.*, p. 1067.
11. Kohlberg, "The Cognitive-Developmental Approach to Moral Education," pp. 1066-1067.

12. Kohlberg and Gilligan, "Adolescent as Philosopher," pp. 1066-1067.
13. Francis Gross, Jr., *Erich Fromm and Vatican Council II Humanistic and Authoritarian Attitudes*, unpublished Ph.D. dissertation, University of Ottawa, 1972, pp. 128-178. This is a thorough treatment of democratic images of the Catholic Church in the writings of Vatican Council II; this Council was in session while the author studied in Europe.
14. Kohlberg and Gilligan, "The Adolescent as Philosopher," pp. 1071-1078.
15. *Ibid.*
16. *Ibid.*
17. *Ibid.*
18. The Gospel according to Mark, 12/28-34. The Book of Deuteronomy, 6/4.

CHAPTER VIII. TEACHING COGNITIVE-MORAL DEVELOPMENT IN COLLEGE

1. Kohlberg's work will be referred to as it comes up in our description.
2. William G. Perry, Jr., *Forms of Intellectual and Ethical Development in the College Years: A Scheme* (New York, 1970).
3. Erik H. Erikson, *Identity: Youth and Crisis*, (New York, 1968). *Childhood and Society* (2nd edition), (New York, 1963).
4. Elisabeth Kubler-Ross, *On Death and Dying* (New York, 1969).
5. Lawrence Kohlberg, "From Is to Ought: How to Commit the Naturalistic Fallacy and Get Away With It," in *Cognitive Development and Epistemology*, edited by Theodore Mischel (New York, 1971), pp. 184-188.
6. *Ibid.*, pp. 186-188. Lawrence Kohlberg and Carol Gilligan, "The Adolescent as Philosopher," *Daedalus*, Fall, 1971, pp. 1062-1063, 1072.
7. Kohlberg, "From Is to Ought," p. 188.
8. *Ibid.*, pp. 155-180.
9. *Ibid.*, pp. 189, 190.
10. *Ibid.*, p. 190 (emphasis mine).
11. *Ibid.*, pp. 191-192.
12. *Ibid.*, p. 193.
13. *Ibid.*, pp. 164-165.
14. *Ibid.*, p. 183.
15. *Ibid.*, p. 186.
16. Lawrence Kohlberg, "The Implications of Moral Stages for Adult Education," *Religious Education*, LXXII; 2 (1977), pp. 197-200.
17. *Ibid.*, p. 199.
18. "Socratic Method," *The Random House Dictionary of the English Language*, Unabridged Edition (New York, 1973).
19. Kohlberg, "From Is to Ought," p. 195 (emphasis mine).
20. *Hunger in America* (New York, Columbia Broadcasting System, 1968).
21. Perry, *op. cit.*

22. Anonymous, "Polarization," *A Handbook of Structured Experiences for Human Relations Training*, Vol. III edited by J. William Pfeiffer and John E. Jones (Iowa City, 1971), pp. 64-68.
23. Maya Angelou, *I Know Why the Caged Bird Sings* (New York, 1969).
24. Anon., "Kerner Report: Seeking Consensus," *Handbook of Structured Experiences*, Vol. III, p. 74. Francis L. Gross, Jr. "Using Small Groups in Undergraduate Teaching," *Perspectives* (now *Interdisciplinary Perspectives*) Vol. 6, No. 2 (1974), pp. 64-75.
25. Perry, *op. cit.*, pp. 177-200.
26. Simon, Howe and Kirschenbaum, *Values Clarification: A Handbook of Practical Strategies for Teachers and Students* (New York, 1972), p. 281-286.
27. Maya Angelou, *op. cit.*, p. 231.
28. Jack Nicholson, director, "A Sense of Purpose," in *Searching for Values, a Film Anthology*. New York: The Learning Corporation of America, 1972.
29. Benjamin S. Bloom, editor, *Taxonomy of Educational Objectives* (New York, 1965).
30. Kohlberg, "From Is to Ought," pp. 164-165.
31. Margaret Craven, *I Heard the Owl Call My Name* (New York, 1973).
32. *Ibid.*, pp. 67-68.
33. Lawrence Kohlberg and Carol Gilligan, "The Adolescent as Philosopher, pp. 1075-1078. In this article Kohlberg and Gilligan acknowledge the light cast on their work by Erikson's study of adolesence.
34. J. D. Salinger, *The Catcher in the Rye*, (New York, 1951).
35. Kubler-Ross, *op. cit.*
36. *Peege*, New York: Phoenix Films, 1974.
37. Kohlberg, "From Is to Ought," p. 188.

CHAPTER IX. THE ASYLUM REVISITED

1. Erik H. Erikson, *Insight and Responsibility* (New York, 1964, p. 124-127.
2. Erik H. Erikson, *Identity: Youth and Crisis* (New York, 1968), pp. 156-157.
3. William G. Perry, Jr., *Forms of Intellectual and Ethical Development in the College Years: A Scheme* (New York, 1970).
4. Erik H. Erikson, *Young Man Luther* (New York, 1958), p. 43.
5. Lawrence Kohlberg, "The Implications of Moral Stages for Adult Education," *Religious Education*, LXXII; 2 (1977), pp. 183-201.
6. Erikson, *Young Man Luther*, p. 14.
7. C. G. Jung, *The Basic Writings of C. G. Jung* (New York, 1937), p. 481.
8. *Ibid.*, p. 501.
9. Erikson, *Identity: Youth and Crisis*, p. 19.

10. Jung, *op. cit.*, p. 502.
11. Erikson, *Identity: Youth and Crisis*, p. 314.
12. Perry, *op. cit.*, Kohlberg, "From Is to Ought," pp. 153-235. L. Theodore Mischel (ed.), *Cognitive Development and Epistomology* (New York, 1971).
13. James W. Fowler, "Stages in Faith: The Structural Developmental Approach," in *Values and Moral Development*, edited by Thomas C. Hennessy (New York, 1976), p. 173-211.
14. Jim Fowler and Sam Keen, Life Maps: *Conversations on the Journey of Faith* (Waco, 1978), pp. 16, 29.
15. James W. Fowler, "Towards a Developmental Perspective on Faith," in *Religious Education*, LXIX; 2 (1974), pp. 207-208.
16. Erikson, *Young Man Luther*, p. 45, ff.
17. James W. Fowler, *Faith and the Structure of Meaning*, 1979, p. 79, p. 18. Unpublished manuscript.
18. Fowler and Keen, *op. cit.*, p. 89.
19. *Ibid.*, p. 138.
20. Erikson, *Identity: Youth and Crisis*, p. 16.

CHAPTER X. A SEQUENTIAL SEXTET (Faith Stages in One Family)

1. James W. Fowler, "Stages in Faith: The Structural Developmental Approach," *Values and Moral Development*, Thomas C. Hennessy, S.J., ed. (New York, 1976), pp. 173-211. James W. Fowler, "Toward a Developmental Perspective on Faith," *Religious Education*, March-April, 1974, pp. 207-219. James W. Fowler, Sam Keen and Philip Berryman, *Life-Maps: Conversations on the Journey of Faith* (Waco, 1978).
2. James W. Fowler, "Stages in Faith," pp. 174-179.
3. Jean Piaget, *The Language and Thought of the Child*, (New York, 1926). The works of Piaget and his commentators are so prolix that this is no place for more than a sample reference.
4. Lawrence Kohlberg, "From Is to Ought," *Cognitive Development and Epistemology*, Theodore Mischel, ed. (New York, 1971), pp. 151-234. This remains my own choice as the most complete exposition of Kohlberg's studies. His works are also too numerous to cite here.
5. Erik H. Erikson, *Childhood and Society*, (2nd ed., New York, 1963), pp. 247-274. I choose this one reference among Erikson's many articles and books because it is not only the earliest reference in book form to his celebrated "eight stages of man," but one of the most succinct.
6. Fowler, "Stages in Faith," pp. 188-189.

7. *Ibid.*, pp. 190-191.
8. Fowler, *Life Maps*, p. 21.
9. Fowler, "Stages in Faith," p. 175.
10. *Ibid.*, p. 177.
11. Fowler, *Life Maps*, pp. 17-18. Fowler, "Faith, Liberation and Human Development," *The Foundation*, Vol. LXXIX, 1974, p. 3-10.
12. Fowler, *Life Maps*, p. 18.

INDEX

215

220